KNIGHT
OF THE
HOLY GHOST

*A Short History of
G. K. Chesterton*

BY DALE AHLQUIST

Published by Ignatius Press and
Faith & Culture Books, an imprint of the Augustine Institute

Ignatius Press Distribution
1915 Aster Rd.
Sycamore, IL 60178
Tel: (630) 246-2204
www.ignatius.com

Augustine Institute
6160 S. Syracuse Way, Suite 310
Greenwood Village, CO 80111
Tel: (866) 767-3155
www.augustineinstitute.org

Cover Design: Christina Gray

ISBN: 978-0-9993756-4-8
Library of Congress Control Number 2018962095

Printed in Canada ∞

To Aidan Mackey
A good and gentle knight

AUTHOR'S NOTE

Portions of this book are revised from articles I have written that previously appeared in *Gilbert!*, *Faith and Reason*, and *Notre Dame Magazine*. I also wish to thank Joseph Pearce, Kevin O'Brien, Sean Dailey, Nancy Brown, Chris Chan, John Peterson, Ron McCloskey, Peter Floriani, Geir Hasnes, John Holland, a bunch of priests, especially Fr. James Schall, Fr. Ian Ker, Fr. Ian Boyd, Fr. Joseph Fessio, Fr. John Udris, and Fr. Spencer Howe, and all the people I've forgotten to mention.

CONTENTS

INTRODUCTION

The Canticle of Sirach

Happy the man who meditates on wisdom,
    and reflects on knowledge;
Who ponders her ways in his heart,
    and understands her paths;
Who encamps near her house,
    and fastens his tent pegs next to her walls;

Who pitches his tent beside her,
    and lives as her welcome neighbor;
Who builds his nest in her leafage,
    and lodges in her branches;
Who takes shelter with her from the heat,
    and dwells in her home.

Motherlike she will meet him,
    like a young bride she will embrace him,
Nourish him with the bread of understanding,
    and give him the water of learning to drink.

He will lean upon her and not fall,
  he will trust in her and not be put to shame.
She will exalt him above his fellows;
  in the assembly she will make him eloquent.
Joy and gladness he will find,
  an everlasting name inherit.

(Sir 14:20–21, 24–27; 15:2–6, NAB)

There are some writers who make us feel smart, and there are some writers who make us feel stupid. Too often a writer makes us feel smart because he is stupid or makes us feel stupid because he is smart, at least smarter than we are. Neither gives us much lasting pleasure. But there are certain writers who make us feel smart because they tell us the truth, and we recognize it as the truth, and we wish we could have said it so well ourselves. We are invigorated by being told what we already know, and we wish everybody else knew it, too. In fact, we think they *do* know it. They just haven't heard it yet. The best writer is the one who gives us something that we want to give to everyone else.

Such a writer is G. K. Chesterton. Here is the wise man described by Sirach, the man who is happy because he meditates on wisdom and makes it his dwelling and then welcomes us in. Chesterton never used his gigantic intellect to crush others or even to take advantage of them, but only to serve something larger than his own large self. Most of his opponents recognized this, which is why they loved him even if they did not agree with him. Most of his friends came to take it for granted, which is why they were able to work alongside him without being over-awed by him. But the average people who encountered him were simply astonished by him. They found him as dazzling as a fireworks show. His fame was widespread. His literary and intellectual achievements were praised across the globe. At the same time, the world did not quite know what to do with him. He did not fit into any of their categories. It is one of the reasons why he managed to utterly disappear in the generation after his death.

But after having been forgotten, G. K. Chesterton is now enjoying a resurgence in popularity. Why? Well, the obvious reason is that people are reading him again. The rediscovery of Chesterton has less to do with his importance as a figure from history than his significance in the present. He has proven himself to be timeless. As his words return to print, we have discovered that he is speaking to us right now. He is talking about all the things we face. He describes the enemy without fear, describes the truth with precision, error with howling laughter, and the battle with an almost raucous joy.

And he's quotable. Maybe you've heard these:

"The Christian ideal has not been tried and found wanting. It has been found difficult and left untried."[1]

"The Bible tells us to love our neighbor and to love our enemy, generally because they are the same people."[2]

"A dead thing can go with the stream, only a living thing can go against it."[3]

"We don't need a Church that moves with the world; we need a Church that moves the world."[4]

"Angels can fly because they can take themselves lightly."[5]

But here are some you probably haven't heard:

"The spirit of the age is very often the worst enemy of the age."[6]

"If you attempt an actual argument with a modern paper of opposite politics, you will . . . have no answer except slanging or silence."[7]

"Satire has weakened in our epoch for several reasons, but chiefly, I think, because the world has become too absurd to be satirized."[8]

"Freedom of speech means practically in our modern civilization that we must only talk about unimportant things."[9]

"Our generation, in a dirty, pessimistic period, has blasphemously underrated the beauty of life and cravenly overrated its dangers."[10]

"The mere strain of modern life is unbearable; and in it even the things that men do desire may break down; marriage and fair ownership and worship and the mysterious worth of man."[11]

"How can it be more important to teach a child how to avoid disease than how to value life?"[12]

"There was a dramatic drop in moral standards on the day they discovered that the test-tube is mightier than the sword."[13]

"A strange fanaticism fills our time: the fanatical hatred of morality, especially of Christian morality."[14]

"There will be more, not less, respect for human rights if they can be treated as divine rights."[15]

"Modern men are not familiar with the rational arguments for tradition, but they are familiar, almost wearily familiar, with all the rational arguments for change."[16]

"If Christianity needs to be 'new,' it does not need to be Christian."[17]

"The terrible danger in the heart of our Society is that the tests are giving way. We are altering, not the evils, but the standards of good by which alone evils can be detected and defined."[18]

"There are many critics who claim that it is morbid to confess your sins. But the morbid thing is *not* to confess them. The morbid thing is to conceal your sins and let them eat away at your soul, which is exactly the state of most people in today's highly civilized communities."[19]

I could go on and on. I often do. Quoting Chesterton is delicious. His words provide exquisite flavor and enormous satisfaction. But what do we especially notice in the above quotations besides how clearly and crisply the truth bursts out of them? They are utterly timely. They describe today. Yet they were written a hundred years ago.

So, who is the man who said these things? All of Chesterton's biographies, especially this brief one, suffer from the same weakness. They cannot capture him. He always manages to escape. We learn of the events of his life, the characters who populated it, his fame, his travels, his conversion. We take in amusing stories of his adventures in pubs or on sidewalks or at after-dinner speeches, and we get a taste of the man, a glimpse, and then he's gone. We never really get to know him as he passes by us.

I think the only way to get to know Gilbert Keith Chesterton is to listen to him talk. To read him is to listen to him talk, for as several people who knew him (including his wife) attested, he talked just like he wrote. The research of the American Chesterton Society has also uncovered hundreds of accounts of his speeches, which also affirm that he talked just like he wrote. I have spent over thirty-six years—the length of Chesterton's literary career—listening to him talk. I feel like I can say that I've gotten to know him. I have certainly become friends with him. And one of the things I've especially learned is that he is a stranger to his critics. They make it evident that they have not listened to him and have not really gotten to know him. They do not read him. They only read *about* him. They get a glimpse, but it is not even an honest glimpse. They're looking at a mask, but they are the ones who have put the mask on him. I am frustrated by how they have misrepresented him, but I am saddened by how they have cheated themselves of the beatitude of being with the man who was Chesterton.

The world we live in is a mess. It does no good to deny it. And it does no good to deny that G. K. Chesterton prophetically described the mess we are in. But he also described why it has happened, and he proposed solutions for cleaning it up. When a prophet has been proved right in his predictions, it is worthwhile to look at his precepts. It is certainly worthwhile to get to know G. K. Chesterton. And so, please allow me to introduce you to a friend of mine. But all I can do is introduce you. You'll have to get to know him yourself.

THE MAN

"Most of those who know me have been able to distinguish me at a glance from a haggard and emaciated genius, starving in a garret and spitting out curses against the critics and the human race." [1]

The concepts of time and space provide unending theoretical riddles for physicists and cosmologists and philosophers and science fiction writers. But for G. K. Chesterton they provided more practical challenges. He seldom knew what time it was, or even what day it was. And, as for space, he acknowledged he took up too much of it, but he was never sure if he was occupying the right space at the right time. He was notorious for being late for his appointments, but he was also known on occasion to be early—by an entire day. He was infamous as well for leaving out dates. He never dated his letters. He wrote a book on the history of England with no dates in it. He wrote several biographies that provide almost nothing of the whens, the wheres, and the whats of the subject's life. And his book *The Everlasting Man* is essentially a history of the world devoid of dates. However, he does concede that dates can occasionally be useful.

So let us begin with this useful date: July 30, 1922.

It was a Sunday. There was no Catholic church in Beaconsfield, England, a quiet little town about thirty miles west of London. We won't call it a historic town because all the towns in England are historic. At the main crossroads of the town stood two pubs, the White Hart and the Saracen's Head. Across from them was the stately former Catholic church, All Saints, which somehow had become Anglican more than three hundred years earlier when the Crown relieved it from its papist occupants. About a mile down the road, just up the hill from the railroad station, stood the Railway Hotel. The hotel was owned by an old couple named Borlase, who permitted a temporary building with a corrugated tin roof to be built adjoining the hotel. Inside this unsightly facade was a Catholic chapel, and on this day and in this place Gilbert Keith Chesterton made his first Confession and a Profession of Faith and was received into the Roman Catholic Church. He was forty-eight years old.

His beloved wife Frances, who was five years his senior, had been expecting this day to come for a long time. Her husband had been defending the Catholic Faith for almost twenty years. His brother Cecil had converted in 1912. When G. K. suffered a nearly complete physical collapse and almost died in 1914, Frances assumed that, if he recovered, he would immediately make the decision to enter the Church. But it did not happen. Something was continuing to prevent him. She did not realize that she was the something. Though she did nothing purposely to stand in his way, she was precisely the reason for his long delay. He could not make so important a step without his companion, the love of his life with whom he shared everything. It was Frances upon whom he depended to fight the challenges of time and space. She would be the one to get him to his meetings and his speaking engagements not only on time but at all. She would take care of the diurnal details in his life, so that this absentminded genius could pour his great thoughts onto paper. At social gatherings, he would be deep in conversation with other guests and suddenly ask, "Where's Frances?" And upon being informed where she was and asked if he needed her, he would respond, "Not right now, but I might." He was comically helpless without her. Once, when traveling alone, he famously got off a train and walked to a telegraph station and wired his wife, "Am at Market Harborough. Where ought I to be?"

But that amusing story illustrates that Gilbert had learned the perils of trying to do anything without Frances, even something so simple as trying to get from one place to the next while traveling alone. To step into the Catholic Church meant that he would be traveling alone, for Frances did not feel the same tug toward Rome that had been pulling him for years. She was quite content to remain a devout Anglican.

Gilbert owed so much to Frances. Besides solving the practical problems of time and space so that he could be the writer he was, she was, much more importantly, the one who played the most important role in him becoming a Christian. He said she was the first Christian he had ever met who was happy. But almost as soon as he entered the Church of England, he wanted to go further. He later called his conversion to Christianity his incomplete conversion to Catholicism. As a literary celebrity, he was also an Anglo-Catholic celebrity, and it was not a role he wanted to play. What he really wanted was to be Catholic. But to take what seemed a short step to Rome was to take a very long step away from Frances. To suddenly not share with his wife the most vital and profound thing in his life was something he could not do. Except one day he finally did. July 30, 1922.

The day was bittersweet. Frances was happy for Gilbert because she knew this was what he wanted. He was happy because he certainly had longed for full communion with the Church, which represented a philosophical and theological and social convergence of all his ideas, the completion of his complete thinking. But they both had tears in their eyes. Gilbert tried to comfort Frances, but he knew even more than she that a separation had come between them.

At the conclusion of the Mass, they went separate ways that day, figuratively and literally. He with the boys (the priests, in this case), and she with the girls (some friends for tea). But he wrote a poem later that day called "The Convert." In it he describes how in one minute his whole life was turned right side up, and the wisdom of this world was less than dust, "for my name is Lazarus, and I live."[2]

Every convert gives something up. As Chesterton said, to choose anything is to reject everything else. Though his conversion should have been the most natural thing in the world, with all of his intellectual strength bearing down on one conclusion, it was painful, as painful as death. But in this Faith, death is followed by resurrection.

Two months later, he was confirmed by Bishop Cary-Elwes of Northampton. Gilbert took as his confirmation name Francis. It was the name of his favorite saint, about whom he would write his first book following his conversion. It was also the name of his wife. In his book on the saint, Chesterton says that, for Francis, religion was not a theory but a love affair, and "there are those who do not believe that a heavenly love can be as real as an earthly love. But I do."[3]

In a sense Chesterton had begun a new love affair, not only with God, but with Frances the woman he now longed for in an entirely new way. He had fallen in love with her in 1896, at a debating society hosted in her home. It was called the IDK Club. What did those initials stand for? I Don't Know. In the summer of 1898, he proposed to her on a picturesque walking bridge over a pond in St. James Park in London. The engagement would last three years while Gilbert struggled to make some money working as a manuscript reader and editor in the offices of publisher Fisher Unwin. In 1899, tragedy visited when Frances's sister Gertrude was struck and killed by a carriage on a London street. Gilbert comforted his fiancée with one beautiful poem after another.

But after death, resurrection. It was during his courtship and engagement, a time that included what seemed a senseless death, that G. K. Chesterton embraced the Christian Faith. We don't know the date he made that decision. It may not have happened on a particular day. We can see in his writing how he was moving toward what he would later describe as "orthodoxy."

Here is another useful date: July 1, 1901. It was the day Gilbert and Frances were married in St. Mary Abbotts Church in the London suburb of Kensington. It was also the bride's birthday. And on that day Gilbert wrote another poem to Frances entitled "Creation Day," which includes the lines:

> Dearest and first of all things free,
> Alone as bride and queen and friend,
> Brute facts may come and bitter truths,
> But here all doubts shall have an end.[4]

But the battle of faith means that doubts do not have an end in this life. In 1908 another tragedy struck. Frances's brother Knollys was "found drowned," i.e. a probable suicide. Gilbert again had to be the rock of comfort for his beloved. But in the immediate aftermath of this horrible event, he published what is perhaps his most joyful book and ringing defense of the Christian Faith, a book incidentally that includes a condemnation of suicide. *Orthodoxy* remains as fresh and original and quotable over a century later. And it is utterly Catholic even though the man who wrote it was not. Yet.

There is a stunning scene of an apparition of the Blessed Virgin in another pre-Catholic work, his epic poem *The Ballad of the White Horse.* The poem is one of his greatest literary accomplishments, and the one he labored over the longest. He had promised the first canto to Charles Masterman, the editor of the *Albany Journal,* who was waiting to go to press with it. Masterman finally turned up personally at Chesterton's London flat to collect the copy. Frances answered the door and explained that Gilbert was still in bed. He was not asleep. He just hadn't bothered to get up. She went and asked her husband if he had the poem for Masterman. He responded. "Oh, I have it. I just haven't written it down." And so, from his bed, he proceeded to dictate the first canto, then called "The Ballad of Alfred," fifteen pages from inside his head, while Masterman wrote it down, and while his wife scrounged up spare pieces of paper from around their flat. He hadn't written it down because he had neglected to get paper. She ended up tearing open envelopes so the insides could be written on. The full epic would be completed about six years later, and when it was published in 1911, he dedicated the masterpiece to Frances, in gratitude to her for bringing the Christian Faith to him.

While most tragedies are sudden, such as the deaths of Frances's siblings, the couple experienced another family tragedy that was slow-moving. Finally the realization set in that Frances was unable to bear children. These two lovers of family life had both dreamed of having seven children. There would be none. They compensated for this by filling their home with other people's children, hosting No-Adults-Allowed parties, which featured such amusements as Gilbert catching buns in his mouth. Their secretaries were like surrogate daughters, as were the Nicholl sisters, daughters of a widow whom they once met on a holiday and who eventually moved to Beaconsfield to be closer to the Chestertons. But the couple's childless partnership made them even more dependent on each other and made Gilbert's decision to convert even more difficult.

In the midst of his conversion, he wrote another epic poem, the lesser known *Ballad of St. Barbara*. It was published in October of 1922, a month after his confirmation. And it was the only other work he dedicated to his wife. The dedicatory poem is a profound tribute to Frances, a celebration of their married life, of the amazing experiences they had shared:

> Life is not void or stuff for scorners:
> We have laughed loud and kept our love,
> We have heard singers in tavern corners
> And not forgotten the birds above:
> We have known smiters and sons of thunder
> And not unworthily walked with them,
> We have grown wiser and lost not wonder;
> And we have seen Jerusalem.[5]

They did indeed see Jerusalem. They had walked where Jesus walked. In the Garden of Gethsemane, the guide said to them, "This is where God said his prayers."[6] They walked along the Via Dolorosa, the road of tears that led to the Cross. They saw the place where Christ died and where he rose again. And it was on the journey home, when stopping in the Italian port of Brindisi, that G. K. Chesterton walked into a Catholic church and looked up at a statue of the Virgin and Child, and there made the decision that upon returning to England he would become Catholic. It was Easter Sunday. After death, resurrection.

He called his conversion "the chief event" of his life. But the surprising thing was how outwardly very little changed. He had defended the Catholic Faith in his writings for years; he would continue to do so. He had already written two dozen Father Brown stories. Nothing changed in terms of his stances on justice for the poor, for the laborer, for the downtrodden. He still fought corruption and greed and misgovernment. He still suffered fools gladly.

And yet everything changed. This was the hinge on which his life turned. After standing at the door of the Church and ushering others in without having entered himself, he finally went in. Now he belonged. Now he was in full communion with the saints.

His conversion was big news, reported all around the world. People were shocked for two reasons. Some were quite sure he already was a Catholic, and some were much more sure he would never become one. "I had never thought it possible."[7] Those were the words of the man who had been one of Chesterton's closest friends for over twenty years, a fellow writer and frequent collaborator, and one known for his outspoken and uncompromising defense of his own Catholic Faith: Hilaire Belloc.

When Chesterton was asked why he became Catholic, he answered, "To get rid of my sins."[8] He says that only the Catholic Church can do that, and that when a man steps out of the confessional, he is only five minutes old. His whole life has started over again.

And what were his sins? Of course, we don't know what he told in the confessional. But it is difficult, very difficult, to imagine Chesterton's sins. By all accounts, that is, the accounts of those who actually knew him, he was a righteous man, of extraordinary virtue. There are simply no stories of his sins. There are a few accusations, which are not the same. The most natural accusation is that the large man was a glutton. But while there are stories of him eating in an absentminded way when food was set before him, there are no tales of him continually tucking into feast after feast. On the contrary, the witnesses attest to how little he ate. His secretary Dorothy Collins, who spent more time with him than any of the other secretaries, was actually amazed by it. When his wife would ask him if he wanted dinner, he would answer, "Oh, I suppose if you're going to have something." A glutton would seem to be someone obsessed with food. G. K. Chesterton hardly thought about it. His weight varied throughout his life, and he reached his greatest size before his physical collapse in 1914 and his death in 1936. It would make sense that his heart was taxed at these times. But his lifelong friend E. C. Bentley said that Chesterton's weight was not due to overeating but to a glandular condition and a problem with fluid retention.[9]

What about those fluids? Didn't he drink too much? He enjoyed the convivial company of friends and fellow journalists especially in his Fleet Street days. The pub was a productive place, full of argument about the issues of the day, as well as laughter and singing. But in spite of the laughter, there was nothing trite about those discussions. They talked about other-worldly subjects as they applied to this world. Sometimes a point is better made when a table can be pounded. Among the topics they debated was the very act of drinking, something traditional and universal and now under attack. Just like religion. "Theology and alcohol are things the nature of which can be easily explained and universally applied," says Chesterton.[10]

He was doing battle with Prohibitionists, which was part of his larger battle with Puritans. He defined Puritanism as "righteous indignation about the wrong things."[11] He defended beer and wine as natural and normal, a "nearly universal custom of mankind,"[12] especially of the most civilized part of mankind. "Let a man walk ten miles steadily on a hot summer's day along a dusty English road, and he will soon discover why beer was invented."[13] But he did not defend cocktails, and the drinks of Prohibition, which seemed to exist only for the purpose of getting drunk. "I have no objection to vodka except that I once tasted it."[14] His preferred drink was what the English call claret, a red Bordeaux, and there is physical evidence of it splashed across some of his manuscripts. "Drink because you are happy," he advised, "never because you are miserable."[15] He praised drink as one of God's good gifts, which, like all the others, should be enjoyed and should not be abused. "There is nothing so good as drink, and nothing so bad as drunkenness."[16]

And the fact is, there are no accounts of Chesterton getting drunk. There is one story of him being tipsy, that is, he tipped, or rather tripped over a flowerpot while walking home in the dark after a party. The fall broke his arm. But one does not need to be drunk to trip over a flowerpot in the dark.

An observation from journalist May Bateman, who visited Chesterton's home, Top Meadow, in 1927, is worth mentioning:

> No one can stay at Top Meadow without realization of how abstemious in food and drink is "G. K." He declares himself "fonder of beer" and more anti-Prohibitionist than ever, but that seems largely a matter of word than of deed! He says he can eat "almost anything," and he never fusses about food, but he eats lightly and almost unnoticingly. His whole manner of life is, in fact, one of amazing simplicity, at home and abroad.[17]

Didn't he smoke too much? He admitted he smoked like a chimney. Once, during an interview, he held up his cigar and said, "A Parnassian pleasure."[18] A Parnassian pleasure is a poetic pleasure, an artistic pleasure, or a pleasure that inspires poetry or art. He said tobacco smoke is "the ichor of mental life,"[19] a reference to the lifeblood of the Greek gods. He called his cigar his muse. "Some men write with a pencil, others with a typewriter. I write with a cigar."[20] It's hard to argue with the cigar's success as Chesterton's muse. You could argue that he smoked too much, but you'd have a hard time arguing that it was a sin. Only a Puritan would say so. You could call it a bad habit, and Chesterton would agree. But he said, "All habits are bad habits."[21]

What we don't have are any bawdy stories. There are no hints of dishonesty, much less lies or thievery. We see a life of happy contentment without covetousness.

There are a few flashes of temper. It has been observed that even the best of us will occasionally take a whip against the moneychangers. For the most part, except in one instance where he unleashed some bitterness after the death of his brother, he expressed his anger with restraint. He had a passion for justice but was not judgmental. He pleaded for what was right without being self-righteous. His humor and his humility would usually defuse tension. Pride was never his problem. He was not selfish. He gave money to the poor, especially to beggars. He gave his time to one charitable venture after another. He treated people fairly. His employees never complained about him. Rather, all of them cherished the time that they worked for him.

Lust? Not here. In a lovely letter to his fiancée, as he is declaring his love for her, he says that "with all his faults," he has never "gone after strange women," that is, he has never strayed into sexual sin. "You cannot think how a man's self-restraint is rewarded in this."[22] Chesterton says elsewhere, "The reward of chastity is a clearness of the intellect."[23] Never was there a better example of someone with a clearness of intellect. He also says, "Purity is the only atmosphere for passion."[24] That's the difference between Puritanism and purity, between lust and love.

Some critics have ridiculously tried to suggest that Chesterton was a "repressed homosexual." Since there is zero evidence that he was an "*un*repressed" homosexual, the claim is a far reach. There are no documents, no testimonies, nothing. Only a few third hand "suggestions." The balkers at Chesterton's purity apparently have never read any of the love poetry he wrote for Frances, or they think it positively hypocritical. Nor do they regard as anything other than a sham his fundamental and pervasive writings about married life and love, of the romance and adventure of husband and wife, of the prince and the princess of the fairy tale, and the king and queen of the home. They also have to disregard the other matter that GKC himself flat out says that he never felt "the faintest temptation to the particular madness of Oscar Wilde."[25] It should be noted as well that Chesterton says it is no great virtue never to commit a sin that one is not tempted to commit.

What was his temptation then? Did he fall into any of the seven deadlies? By his own account, yes. It was sloth. But even here, one must beware the credibility of the source.

Though there was a time in his life and career when he took long walks, which is a good way to think, especially if one is a writer, he tended to the sedentary life. He hated exercise. He even argued against exercise for exercise's sake, just as he argued against art for art's sake—it should be for the sake of something else. He said one should ride horses or play games, and thus get exercise by doing something else. But he didn't ride horses, and the physical games he played seem to be limited to such things as croquet, hide the slipper, and catching buns in his mouth. He said he once played golf "before it became a religion."[26] He would walk about in his garden throwing a javelin or Indian clubs. His secretary, Dorothy Collins, owned a car, something that Chesterton never owned, and in his later years, he would suggest that in the evening Dorothy take them for a ride in the country "for exercise."

But this is not the sloth he was talking about when he said he was guilty of sloth. He was always worried that he was neglecting his duty, his work. Of course, he worked sitting down. His work was writing. And the fact is, he worked and worked. His typical day consisted of eight to ten hours of writing. (And part of writing was dictating to his secretary, which meant strolling back and forth in his study, stabbing at pillows with his swordstick, or firing a bow and arrow out the window.) When he traveled, he was writing. When he was at the pub, he was writing. He would stop in the middle of a staircase or a crowded street to write. When he ran out of paper, he would write on his shirt cuffs. He was always writing. He was one of the most prolific writers who ever lived. A hundred books, thousands of essays, hundreds of poems. He edited two newspapers. He gave hundreds of speeches. He served as chairman of dozens of literary societies, arts and theater groups, charitable organizations, public interest leagues, and political reform committees. One observer said that ninety out of a hundred men could not do a tenth of what Chesterton did. And yet he was afraid that he was giving in to sloth because he always felt he should be doing more, that he was never doing enough. There was still a whole library inside of him, waiting to be written. The twenty years he spent as an editor, laboring over two papers dedicated to bringing justice to an unjust world, took enormous energy and time. And those who knew him best were pained that he was not using his great talent to produce more great literature for the world, literature that would outlast the ephemeral journalism into which he was pouring his efforts. And yet it was during this time that he wrote three of his greatest books: *St. Francis of Assisi*, *St. Thomas Aquinas*, and *The Everlasting Man*. All of them everlasting works.

So, he does not seem even to be guilty of the sin to which he admitted being guilty.

But wait a minute, didn't he hate the Jews? Isn't that a sin? It is. It's a sin to hate anyone. The only problem with this accusation against Chesterton is that it is not true. He did not hate the Jews. Chesterton's "sin" was to mention the Jews. If he had never done this, his critics would have no hay to make.

The fact is, Chesterton had some public run-ins with some prominent Jews. But no one ever wants to discuss his relationships with less-prominent Jews, his rallying to their causes, his friendships, his deep affection for what he called a "gifted and historic race."[27] He said "the world owes God to the Jews."[28] Not something an anti-Semite would proclaim. He traveled to the Holy Land at the invitation of a group of Zionists who were grateful for his support in trying to re-establish a

Jewish homeland. Chesterton accurately portrayed the Jewish people as a nation without a country, but it was distasteful to many that he would refer to them as foreigners. To the cynics who sneered that Chesterton supported Zionism only to rid Europe of the Jews, he replied pointedly that he would "probably die defending" the last Jew in Europe,[29] a response they never seemed to acknowledge, then or now. He was pained but also puzzled at the ugly accusation because he knew that anyone who knew him knew he bore the Jews no malice.

Fr. Brocard Sewell, who as a young man worked for Chesterton at *G. K.'s Weekly*, said that he never witnessed any anti-Semitism from Chesterton.[30] There was no general hatred or hostility toward the Jews or toward any group of people. But he said there were two particular Jews he did not like: Sir Rufus Isaacs and Sir Alfred Mond. The first he considered a corrupt and conniving politician, the second a corrupt and conniving businessman, both of whom had bought their titles and used their positions of power and prestige to advance their personal interests under the guise of being loyal Englishmen. If Chesterton can be criticized for his public denouncement of two particular Jews, then he must also be praised for his defense or his praise of particular Jews. He saved Steinie Morrison, a Jew convicted of murder, from the gallows. He dedicated two of his books, including a volume of Father Brown stories, to Jewish friends. He lauded the work of Israel Zangwill, who similarly praised Chesterton. He invited a Jewish woman in Beaconsfield to help him start a local theatrical troupe. Margaret Halston hesitated because of his "reputation," but after working with him and getting to know him, she realized that his reputation as an anti-Semite was all nonsense. The false charge will continue to be repeated. But it will continue to be a false charge.

Okay, maybe not the Jewish thing, but wasn't Chesterton a racist? After all, he used the n-word! The unforgivable sin. Case closed.

Well, not so fast. To see the n-word in print these days is always something of a shock, but it is important to know that the word was not as politically charged in Chesterton's day (especially in England) as it is today (especially in America). It is now a more-or-less forbidden word (let's just say more—unless it's used for effect in the movies, like every other so-called forbidden word). Chesterton obviously would not use it now. It is clear from his writing and his personality that he would never knowingly or willingly give offense. If you consult the *Century Dictionary*, 1911 edition, you will note that word was used in England "without opprobrium . . . to refer to members of the negro race." *Without opprobrium.* Chesterton's use of the word is not meant to be contemptuous, which of course is how it is now understood no matter how it is meant. He used it interchangeably with the term "negro" or "black man," sometimes within the same sentence. In any case, you must consider Chesterton's writings as a whole. He argued against the inhumanity of black slavery—and all slavery. He explicitly affirmed the brotherhood of all men. "The brotherhood of men is a fact: which in the long run wears down all other facts."[31] This is confirmed by his lifelong friend Bentley, who said of Chesterton:

> To him all men were brothers, not because he held it as an opinion, but because he felt it as a fact in his own case. That was for him the sole and all sufficient basis of democracy, which he held to have for its one foundation the dogma of the divine origin of man.[32]

And perhaps more than any of his contemporaries, Chesterton violently abhorred racial theories of any kind, but especially any idea that suggested the superiority of one race over another. This is evident throughout his writings, in his defense of freedom and democracy, in his praise of the common man, and especially when he took on the modern German racial theories that culminated in Nazism. He said on many occasions that racial theories are complete nonsense. He further argued that the modern racial theories are based on Darwinism, which was being used to prove "scientifically" that blacks were inferior to whites. Chesterton warned the world about giving science too much authority, because the results would be immoral. Racial theories were just one example. Eugenics were another.

Chesterton also decried the lynchings that were still taking place in the American South during his lifetime. He called it a real blot on America, a country which he otherwise admired in many ways because of its democratic spirit. In his book *What I Saw in America*, he wrote: "I believe . . . that the enslavement and importation of negroes ha[s] been the crime and catastrophe of American history."[33] He found it incredible that in America there really was a race war, where people hated each other for no other reason than skin color.

Anyone calling Chesterton a racist should consider the scene he deliberately inserted into his play *The Judgment of Dr. Johnson*, about the great eighteenth-century man of letters Dr. Samuel Johnson, to whom Chesterton himself is often compared. Dr. Johnson uses the n-word several times in the play. But when the American colonists in the room start talking about "freedom for all," Dr. Johnson brings his black servant, Francis "Black Frank" Barber, into the room and serves him tea, to the astonishment of the onlookers. While serving tea to his own servant, he explains to the others that he has left his entire estate to Mr. Barber (which is a historical fact). The Americans are naturally quite embarrassed by their hypocrisy and self-righteousness.

It is true that the n-word appears in other places in Chesterton's fiction and non-fiction, and of course I wish that it did not. But I will challenge anyone to a debate who calls Chesterton a racist. Take away the few instances of the word (and there are only a few), and you simply have no argument at all. On the contrary, you can only find evidence that Chesterton condemned racism and upheld the dignity of all people, whatever their race.

In his Father Brown story "The God of the Gongs," there is an arrogant black character who prompts the comment from Father Brown's companion, Flambeau: "Sometimes I am not surprised that they are lynched."

Father Brown responds: "I am never surprised by any work of hell."

Notice how Flambeau translates his own repugnance of another man's behavior to a repugnance of that other man's race. Father Brown's response reflects Chesterton's own attitude toward racism and racial hatred, and it shows how his ideas go much further than most other modern critics: Racism is a work of Hell; it is evil. It is not just a cultural misunderstanding that can be corrected by education; it is a sin that can only be corrected by repentance.

Maisie Ward, Chesterton's official biographer, long after her two GKC biographies were written, said that in his personal life, Chesterton's approach to race was simply to ignore racial differences. She experienced this firsthand when she stayed at Chesterton's home and was asked to share a room with a black woman. This had never happened to her before. This was in the 1920s, and such a thing was unheard of at that time even in England, where the races did not mix and where prejudice and discrimination were practiced unconsciously. Chesterton did not pay mere lip service to his creed. He lived it. And his writings, in spite of his occasional use of the dreaded word, are simply not racist. "White men," he said, have "behaved like white devils to black men."[34] Racists don't talk like that.

The uninformed attempts to portray the jovial and charitable Chesterton as having a dark side as a Jew-hater or a racist are nasty knocks on his character, but more than that they detract from the real dark side to Chesterton. Because there was indeed a dark side. It was something that he experienced as a young man. There was one great sin to which he was tempted. The sin that Chesterton called not only a sin, but *the* sin.[35]

But in order to talk about that great sin, we need to back up a bit. We have, after all, begun this story in the middle. We might even say we have begun it at its turning point. What led up to Chesterton's conversion?

The first thing that happened to him was being born. That would involve another date worth mentioning—May 29, 1874. He suddenly found himself in the London suburb of Kensington, in a house inhabited by loving middle-class parents named Edward and Marie and an older sister named Beatrice. The sister would tragically die at age eight, but a new sibling, in the form of a younger brother named Cecil, would come along when Gilbert was five years old. Mr. Edward Chesterton worked in the family real estate office a few blocks away. He was an amateur artist, and his study was cluttered with drawings and sculptures and an elaborate toy theater. Gilbert not only got his creative traits from his father but also his kindheartedness. From his mother he got his wit. The parents had no creedal faith but irregularly attended a non-conformist chapel and listened to sermons from the Rev. Stopford Brooke. They considered themselves something along the lines of Unitarian Universalists. They encouraged inquisitiveness in their sons, and the walls of their house were lined with heavily-laden bookshelves. Gilbert showed an early aptitude for literature, devouring Dickens especially, but also Robert Louis Stevenson, Wilkie Collins, Charles Kingsley, and Robert Browning. "I remember in my boyhood Browning kept us awake like coffee."[36] He also read piles of penny dreadfuls and whole volumes of *Chamber's Encyclopaedia*. He had, he said, "a mere brute pleasure of reading, a pleasure in leisurely and mechanical receptiveness. It was the sort of pleasure that a cow must have in grazing all day long."[37] He also loved Shakespeare both on the stage and on the page, and greatly looked forward to the yearly ritual of a new Gilbert and Sullivan production. But all theater appealed to him, from the Christmas pantomime to the cardboard cutouts he would move about inside his toy theater. He put pen to paper early on, both writing and drawing. Yes, he once fancied being an artist, but he never gave the graphic arts as much of his creative energy as he did the literary arts. He was a compulsive and comical doodler, defacing entire textbooks with his drawings, but seldomly produced a finished work of art. Yet he loved to look at art. His earliest published essays were art reviews. One of his earliest books was about the painter G. F. Watts. He would go to art galleries and lose himself in the paintings. Of Botticelli's *Nativity* that hung in the National Gallery, he wrote in one of his childhood notebooks:

> Do you blame me that I sit hours before this picture?
> But if I walked all over the world in the time
> I should hardly see anything worth seeing that is not in
> this picture.[38]

It is not hard to imagine that a young man who could step into a painting and look around could also step easily in and out of Elfland and see everything that there is to see.

He attended St. Paul's school, where about three centuries earlier, John Milton was a student. Gilbert and a small group of friends formed the Junior Debating Club, where each week these fourteen-year-old boys would present papers on English literature. They even published their own paper, which was eagerly purchased by members of the faculty. The boys in the group, half of whom were Jewish, continued to meet regularly throughout their school years and became friends for life. Young Gilbert proposed as a motto for the club, a line from an essay by

William Hazlitt: "Words are the only things that last forever."
Besides their regular debates, they would get together for chess,
for drawing, and for nature hikes.

His closest friend in the group was Edmund Clerihew Bentley,
who invented the poetic form called after his middle name,
and the boys perfected the humorous rhyming biographies
whose biographical information is not necessarily useful or even
accurate. The first one, from Bentley:

> Sir Humphrey Davy
> Detested gravy.
> He lived in the odium
> Of having discovered sodium.

A subsequent one from Chesterton:

> The people of Spain think Cervantes
> Worth half a dozen Dantes
> An opinion opposed most bitterly
> By the people of Italy.

Bentley would go on to become an accomplished journalist
in his own right and the author of the classic detective novel
Trent's Last Case. All of the members of the Junior Debating
Club would go on to Oxford and Cambridge, except for one,
the one that they all acknowledged was the genius of the
group: Gilbert Keith Chesterton. He had never been a very
good student. In fact, the only reason he was able to advance
to the next level one year was that he won the school's coveted
Milton Prize for poetry. But the headmaster at St. Paul's had
told Edward and Marie not to bother sending him to university;
it was impossible to teach him anything.

So, he went to art school. He attended the Slade School of
Art, which was connected to the University of London, where he
also took a few classes in literature and history before dropping

out in his second year. It was at Slade School, he said, where he had the good fortune to discover that he could never be an artist. And also that he could never be a scholar.

But it was during this time, when his close friends were off to college away from London, when he was quite alone, that he sank into a deep depression, and also had more than one encounter with evil. It was the Gay '90s, which were anything but happy. Decadence had begun to creep into art; the lines were becoming blurred. Clear truth was being replaced by vague "impressions," the beauty of romance by stark realism that focused on dirt and warts, and the only political triumph of the day was that of the strong over the weak. A snake had slithered into philosophy and asserted itself in the form a question mark.

Chesterton said that he believed in the devil before he believed in God. He had dabbled in spiritualism, playing about with a planchette (the equivalent of a Ouija board), and had some creepy experiences. But it got worse. He peered deeper into the darkness. And the devil coaxed him to the very edge of the abyss. He was tempted to what he would later call the ultimate act of selfishness, "the ultimate sin."[39] Suicide.

Chesterton would go on to write about suicide in a manner that some have criticized as being callous and unsympathetic to those who suffer from depression. But he was anything but unsympathetic. He went through that kind of depression himself, but he would not refrain from condemning a terrible act whatever its pitiable motivation. And he had to condemn categorically the person he was and what he almost did.

The thing that saved him was "clinging to one thin thread of thanks."[40] Thankfulness is the antithesis of selfishness. It was just enough to pull him out of the pit. He would never return to that place.

There was one other thing that saved him. Walt Whitman. He found Whitman to be "a good ogre"[41] whose positive view of life was exactly what he needed to read. "I hated Swinburne's pessimism as I loved Whitman's optimism."[42] His love of Whitman was later "balanced by better things."[43] And, for anybody wondering about it, he did not know about Whitman's homosexuality (as he put it, discreetly, he "did not discover the more painful controversies"[44]) until he was much older, at which point Whitman's influence no longer played a role in his life. In fact, he became an open critic of free verse. But there is no denying that Whitman gave him an appreciation of the created world so that he wanted "to digest the very rocks and mountains and jungles,"[45] which helped deliver him from his depression. He was also drawn to another figure who would prove to be a permanent friend after his fascination with Whitman faded. Someone else who helped him be thankful for the gift of creation: St. Francis of Assisi. But at this point, he had "no more notion of being a Catholic than of being a Cannibal."[46]

He began to build a philosophy. It began with the axiom that existence is better than nonexistence. From that starting point a very good philosophy can be constructed, one founded on life.

As he began his recovery, he had another encounter with evil, this in the form of a devil-worshipper, a diabolist, a young man who had totally given himself over to evil, willing to try and do anything no matter how forbidden or repulsive. It happened one night during his time at art school. The two art students stood outside in a courtyard warming themselves next to a fire. The other young man suddenly turned to Chesterton and asked when he had become "orthodox." Gilbert realized for the first time that this was indeed the case. He was defending a truth he could not yet articulate and a God he did not yet know. But he knew he no longer belonged to the devil, which was the case with the young man standing on the other side of the flame, a young man who would sadly yield to the same temptation that had drawn Gilbert. He would eventually kill himself. The last time Gilbert saw him was that night. As Chesterton walked away he looked at the fire. He did not know if it was Hell or "the furious love of God."[47] It was both. But the devil could not claim him. God did.

Not long after this he had a very different encounter, not with a demon but with an angel, who came in the form of Frances. He not only found his mate, he found his faith. And he found the other important thing that would make him complete—his vocation. He knew he wanted to be a writer. His ideas were coming together and so was his entire life.

Very few people can actually make their living as a writer. Selling your words is no easy task. You not only have to have something to say, you have to be able to say it well enough so that someone will pay you to say it.

How did he become a writer? He had a gift for language certainly and a mind bursting with creative energy. But he also practiced. In addition to those essays he wrote for the Junior Debating Club, he filled notebooks with stories and plays and poems, and also drew a lot of sketches, mostly of sword fights. There were many ambitious beginnings that were not brought to completion, outlines for plays and novels that were followed by nothing more than an opening scene or paragraph. A poem would end half-formed, a sentence half-written. Sometimes even a word stopped in the middle. He did eventually write an entire novel, but it would not be published until more than a hundred years after he wrote it. Along with his fiction, he nurtured the art of persuasive rhetoric. Thanks to his brother Cecil, he developed the skill of arguing, and apparently had to practice every day.

The only job he ever had before he became a writer also involved books. He worked as a reader at two different publishing houses, sifting through literally thousands of manuscripts. When it came time to make his move to break into print himself, he started by writing some anonymous book reviews and letters to editors. Most of the letters went unnoticed, but the book reviews gained attention quickly. He reviewed books of various quality, and no matter how bad the book was, the review was good. That is not to say it was a good review of the book, but that it was a good review to read that may or may not have had anything to do with the book being reviewed. He read books that no one will ever read again. It is questionable if some of these books were ever read the first time. But he read enough of them to quote from them and express an opinion of them, and then would use them as a launching pad to expound on an idea that was mentioned in the book. If the book in question was about Robert Louis Stevenson, Chesterton would not discuss the book, he would discuss Stevenson. If the book made a passing reference to skeletons, Chesterton's whole essay was about skeletons. Skeletons are good things to have. He seldom trashed a book even if the book was trash. Literature is always a portal to eternity, to timeless ideas that offer endless light.

His anonymous reviews were soon appended with the initials "G. K.C.," and people started asking who it was that was attached to these initials. They would soon find out. In the first year of the twentieth century, his father underwrote the printing of two books of his poetry, *Greybeards at Play* and *The Wild Knight*. In 1901 a real publisher brought out a collection of his essays, *The Defendant*. And then the literary world was shocked in 1903 when he was commissioned to write a monograph on the poet Robert Browning. Chesterton went from being that anonymous book reviewer to being a regular columnist in the *Daily News* and developed a faithful and substantial following, so much so that sales of the paper doubled on the days his column appeared. That year he made another loud splash when he took on editor Robert Blatchford, a well-known atheist, in an ongoing debate in print on the subject of Christianity, which Blatchford had been backhanding. Chesterton defended the Christian Faith, not in one of the religious papers, but in a daily newspaper in the secular press. In 1905 another book came out, *Heretics*, in which he took on the leading thinkers of the day and explained what was wrong with their thinking. Implied in his criticisms of these various skeptics and agnostics was a further defense of Christianity. What was amazing was that he made friends with all these philosophical opponents. They actually sought him out. There was something different about this young writer, and they recognized it. He was as witty as they were, but represented an intelligent and articulate view of God, not easily dismissed or dismantled. Instead, he'd had the audacity to dismiss their own blasphemy as merely an artistic effect and dismantle their own unreasonable antics attempting to reduce religion to a superstition. He showed that they had a superstitious credulity in science and "progress" and "efficiency" and that their agnosticism was not a sign of intelligence but, as the word literally meant, ignorance. "The doubts of a materialist are not worth a dump."[48] His challenges had the paradoxical effect of drawing his opponents in. They wanted to be around him for the intellectual sparks of his discussion and the enjoyment of his companionship. Thus, he became friends with H.G. Wells and George Bernard Shaw and Max Beerbohm and nearly everyone else.

Heretics was a triumph of controversy, but it was followed by an even greater triumph the following year—his masterpiece of literary criticism, *Charles Dickens*. Almost single-handedly Chesterton spurred a huge revival of interest in Dickens, who was fading from popularity. He would go on to write introductions to each of the Dickens novels in newly published editions. In the meantime, Chesterton was hired as a regular columnist for the *Illustrated London News*, which not only gave him a steady income, but a regular platform for his ideas, and, most notably, official recognition as one of London's most important writers. In his next book, he took on one of the greatest living writers in

England, his new friend the playwright Shaw. The book opens with the rather bold statement: "Most people either say that they agree with Bernard Shaw or that they do not understand him. I am the only person who understands him, and I do not agree with him." Shaw called it the best book that he had ever provoked.

Chesterton's next important book was *Orthodoxy*, followed by *What's Wrong with the World*, both of which we shall discuss in the next chapter. In between came three novels: *The Napoleon of Notting Hill*, *The Man Who Was Thursday*, and *The Ball and the Cross*. His novels are truly novel. They don't easily compare with anything that came before or since. His characters are all entertaining, but they all tend to talk like Chesterton, no matter which side of the fence they are on. The narratives lack a lot of detailed description, but the images are vivid. The plots are unbelievable but completely engaging. And though they clearly make a point and have a conclusion, one never quite knows what to make of the endings.

In 1911 came the epic poem *The Ballad of the White Horse*, followed the next year by the first collection of Father Brown stories, featuring the priest-sleuth who immediately carved out a permanent place in detective fiction. The next year his play *Magic* opened on London's West End to rave reviews and played to packed houses for months, followed by a successful run on Broadway. Thus, in a little over a decade Chesterton established himself as a major poet, a novelist, a journalist, a literary critic, a social critic, a philosopher, a Christian apologist, a popular mystery writer, and a successful playwright.

In the years that followed, Chesterton was able to sell not only his written words but his spoken words as well. After several talks to small, local groups in London and southern England, he was invited to speak at a major event, the Anglican Church Congress in Liverpool in October of 1904. This was in the wake of his (newly-won) fame from the Blatchford debates. There were 1,600 people in the audience. He had never faced such a large crowd. His topic was "Aggressive Infidelity." He set in place the ideas that would lead him for the rest of his career: The more aggressive the Christian Church is, the better. It is faith that should be aggressive, not doubt. There is no such thing as a real agnostic; the nearest thing you can get is a newborn babe. Christianity is rational. The idea that there could be a conflict between science and religion is absurd.

He won everyone over.

He was suddenly in great demand as a public speaker, giving hundreds and hundreds of talks all around England, and would eventually go on speaking tours to other countries, including France, Spain, the Netherlands, Poland, Palestine, Italy, and America. Wherever he traveled, it was front page news in the local press, and the lecture halls were always full. He was famous not only for his words but for his character and his distinctive appearance. Large. Long hair. Mustache. Pince-nez hanging crookedly on his nose. Great cape. Slouch hat. Walking stick.

"Everybody seems to know you, Mr. Chesterton."

"If they don't," he sighed to the young lady on the street, "they ask."[49]

People on the sidewalk would part like the Red Sea before him. He would move forward, his brow furrowed "in an agony of concentration," thinking the next thought that was about to make its way to paper. He would stand in the middle of the street, oblivious of traffic, lost in an idea, or rather, found in one. He had the uncanny ability to think out loud with a complete lack of self-consciousness. And the rest of the world would listen in. He could be seen sitting in a pub, laughing over the page he was writing, shaking the rafters. "Damn, that's good!" He considered it haughty not to laugh at one's own jokes. "May not an architect pray in his own cathedral?"[50] He could also be counted on to stop at every bookstall and newspaper stand, with the demeanor of one of his own fictional detectives looking for a clue.

Though he loved London, he deliberately moved away. It was in 1909 when Gilbert and Frances relocated to the town of Beaconsfield, something they had actually dreamed of doing since they got married. Their first house was called Overroads and was uniquely shaped with three wings, but they eventually constructed an even more unusual home across the road called Top Meadow. The first room built was a large studio with a stage at one end and a balcony at the other. The rest of the house was slowly erected around it. Chesterton said that St. Francis was a poet whose whole life was a poem. The same could be said of himself, but it might be even more accurate to say that Chesterton was a child whose whole life was a toy theater. He played the role of St. George and was always slaying dragons and rescuing princesses. His lance was a pen. He was the wild knight.

His childlike qualities are revealed in his love to play dress-up. He dressed up as Dr. Johnson, as Father Christmas, as Sam Weller (from Dickens's *Pickwick Papers*), as Old King Cole. These were always connected to local pageants. There is a certain ceremony to dressing up. He said that ceremony goes with innocence. "Children are not ashamed of dressing-up, nor great poets at great periods, as when Petrarch wore the laurel." But the most interesting character he dressed up as was G. K. Chesterton. He wore the same costume for most of his career. He was expected to wear it. He clearly enjoyed wearing it. He enjoyed dressing up as himself.

Though he made friends with almost all of his enemies, Chesterton made one great literary enemy who died hating him. It was Thomas Hardy. In his 1913 book *The Victorian Age in Literature*, Chesterton makes the remark, almost off-handedly, that Thomas Hardy was "a sort of village atheist brooding and blaspheming over the village idiot." That succinct piece of literary criticism stuck to Hardy, and he could not shake the image for the rest of his life. He died railing against Chesterton, having written an infantile poem on his deathbed still trying to rebut the charge. There are two ironies about this. First, Chesterton's description is completely accurate, which is why it clung to Hardy so well. He hated it but what did he expect? He was a cold and quiet unbeliever who picked up his pen and wrote beautiful indulgent prose about how cruel life is, luxuriating in his bitterness at the God whom he loathes for not existing and exacting his revenge by describing the details of the miserable lives of the creatures he didn't create. It seems that what Hardy really hated most was that Chesterton was happy and Hardy was not. The second irony is that Chesterton never even knew that Hardy felt this way about him, that he obsessed over him all the way to his grave. Chesterton might have known that Hardy was at odds with him because Hardy was at odds with God. Chesterton criticized Hardy's skepticism and pessimism but admired his craftsmanship. There is actually a third irony. Chesterton, still oblivious to Hardy's hatred of him, spoke up on Hardy's behalf about the fact that his last wishes were not honored. He wanted to be buried on his own land and not in Westminster Abbey.

> He was a man whose first principles of philosophy had all gone wrong; but whose last lingering traditions and tastes and instincts had remained radically and tenaciously right. . . . He had 'the vertigo of the infinite' about all the ultimate things. But he never lost his love for the nearest things. Whatever else he was, he was a local patriot; and he ought to have been buried like a patriot, within the frontiers of his small nationality. . . . Instead of being used to dignify Wessex, he has been used to vulgarize Westminster Abbey. For, although

Hardy himself was the very reverse of vulgar, this particular sort of boom about burials really is vulgar. It is a third-rate sort of thing to make a fuss about a man being put in Westminster Abbey, as if it were about his being put in Madame Tussaud's.[51]

Chesterton also pointed out the troubling detail that the Abbey was in fact once an abbey. "The truth is that we cannot do anything with a national religious building without a national religion."[52] It explains, in part, why Chesterton is not himself enshrined in the Poet's Corner.

In the second decade of the twentieth century, Chesterton's great popularity and success veered slightly off course due to two major tragedies in his life, both of which involved his brother Cecil. The first was connected to what was known as the Marconi Scandal, which will be dealt with in the next chapter, and the second was Cecil's death, which will also have to wait till the next chapter. GKC wrote about the former with an unresolved anger throughout the rest of his life, the latter in only one bitter outburst. Ironically, it was in the midst of the Marconi Scandal that he wrote his most rollicking and uproarious novel, *The Flying Inn*, with its comical characters and lighthearted drinking songs. There were two other major disruptive events during this decade that took him somewhat out of the limelight, but he would have considered these secondary to the other two. One of them was the First World War, which consumed him for four years, and the other was his own very close brush with death. As for the former, Chesterton is criticized for what seems to be an unnatural and unrelenting hatred of Germany. But it was not Germany he hated. He defended the right of a nation to be itself. What he hated was an unnatural thing that was not a nation, but a bad idea. It was called Prussia. His hatred of Prussia is explained in part by his love of Belgium. He had firsthand accounts of the atrocities committed by German soldiers when they seized Belgium, which is one of the main things that prompted England's entry into the war. The treatment of the Belgians was an outrage. It had "the stunning directness of a blow from hell."[53] But what also outraged GK was the very idea of one country invading another and simply taking it over, claiming it for itself. It was especially poignant because only a few years earlier he had visited Belgium, enjoying the simple pleasures of its small towns. It was, he says, "a scene of peace and prosperity." It had been obscenely destroyed by Prussia's unprovoked invasion. But shortly after the war began, G. K. Chesterton's own life almost came to an end. In the fall of 1914, he was giving a lecture when he became faint and disoriented. He made his way home and collapsed on the bed, causing the bed to collapse as well. Then his body started to shut down, and he was semi-comatose for almost six months. He started to come out of it during Easter of 1915. The exact nature of the malady has never been determined, but he made a complete recovery, picked up his lance, got back on his saddle, and charged back into battle with full energy. But his world before the war and after the war were two different worlds. Just as Europe was two different worlds before and after. A life of creative opportunity and blossoming excitement was visited by death and disappointment and the stench of corruption. But after death, resurrection. By the end of the decade, he was not only back in form, but back to his former prominence.

He traveled to Ireland in 1918 and to the Holy Land in 1919. Each trip produced a book. Chesterton argued that the Irish were a distinct people from the English and deserved their autonomy, to be able to rule their own country in their own way, to protect their traditions and their religion. For that he has always been recognized as a defender of human rights and freedom in general and a champion of the Irish in particular. However, when he made the exact same arguments on behalf of the Jews, he was called anti-Semitic.

His first trip to America was in 1921. When he stepped off the boat, he said he had come in order to lose his impressions of America. He told the press he did not plan to write a book about America. Apparently that plan did not work out. The book came out a year later. He said New York reminded him of… Hell, "pleasantly of course," and he observed famously that the lights of Broadway would have been beautiful "if only one could not read." While he said he felt at home in both Ireland and Palestine, he said that in the United States, he really felt as if he "were on another planet." But perhaps the best comment on America came from his wife, a comment that went unreported for years until Gilbert quoted it himself. When Frances first tasted tea in America she remarked, "Well, if that's the sort of tea we sent you, I don't wonder you threw it into Boston Harbor."[54]

On his speaking tour, Chesterton rotated three lectures: "The Perils of Health," "Shall We Abolish the Inevitable?" and "The Ignorance of the Educated," but each talk was unique as is indicated by the reports. The tour took him to Boston, Philadelphia, and upstate New York (affording him a look at Niagara Falls), up into Canada to Ottawa, where he visited relatives, to Toronto and Montreal, back into the United States, through the midwest to Detroit, Madison, Minneapolis, Duluth, Omaha, Chicago, Cleveland, Columbus, Kansas City, St. Louis, Oklahoma City, Nashville, Indianapolis, and back to New York City. He was hosted by mayors and governors and literary and society figures.

While he was generally lauded by both the press and the public, there was one exception. The *Omaha Bee* went after him as being utterly incomprehensible. However, the Creighton University paper went after the *Omaha Bee*, defending

Chesterton and chiding the locals for rising to the stereotype of being yokels.

He was also taken to task by one reporter who criticized "The Ignorance of the Educated" talk, pointing out that GKC had wrongly attributed the line "It ain't so much mens' ignorance that does the harm as their knowing so many things that ain't so" to Artemus Ward, when it came from Josh Billings. However, the reporter didn't quite get it right either. What Josh Billings actually said was "I honestly beleave it iz better tew know nothing than two know what ain't so." Chesterton would continue to quote the line incorrectly but would correctly attribute it to Josh Billings. The misquote, of course, is better. Chesterton usually misquoted authors to their advantage.

More than one account described him as "a big, bashful boy" who would crack one joke after another, drawing increasing laughter from those around him. But he would also laugh spontaneously at his own quips, "with the innocent surprise of one who has just discovered something unusually funny, and can hardly wait to tell others about it."[55]

A reporter in Baltimore said that Chesterton "talks like one of his own brilliant essays,"[56] and Tennessee poet John Crowe Ransom said he was the best lecturer he had ever heard.[57]

In his lectures, he criticized the modern world's unthinking slavery to fads and discussed the things it loses rather than gains from technology, the things it has forgotten from history, and its general lack of common sense. "The world is not so anxious to do things worth doing as to do things not worth doing, and do them very well."[58]

At the conclusion of one of his lectures in Philadelphia, a woman stood and asked, "What do you consider the weakest point in our civilization?" She sat down and waited with the rest of the audience for a dissertation on religion or government, but Chesterton chuckled and simply answered, "Well, I have always felt that it is the duty of every one of us to consider himself the weakest point."[59]

In Ardmore, Oklahoma, he attended a famous murder trial. A millionaire senator, Jake Hamon, was shot to death by a young woman he had seduced. She was acquitted. GKC made the national news by saying that she would have been hanged in England. It was not that he would have endorsed such a verdict. He went so far as to say that he would have preferred that she had been murdered by the senator, which would have made a good detective story, leading to the proper hanging of a millionaire.[60]

In Cleveland, he told the press that it was distressing to contemplate how few politicians are hanged.[61]

One thing that he had hoped to see in the American West was a "Red Indian." But he didn't. On his second trip to America ten years later, he was similarly disappointed. The first time he saw one was in 1932 in Dublin at the Eucharistic Conference. And the Indian happened to be a Roman Catholic priest.

He lectured at Yale in New Haven, Connecticut, which is also the headquarters of the Knights of Columbus. There, the Knights presented him with a snakewood walking stick, which became a prized possession, the one he chose that July morning the following year when he walked to the tin shed to be received into the Catholic Church.

Upon his departure, the New York press asked him what most impressed him about America. He answered, "The number of people who came to my lectures."[62] On the ship returning to England, he met explorer Ernest Shackleton, Florenz Ziegfield of the Ziegfield Follies and his wife Billie Burke (who played Glinda the Good Witch in *The Wizard of Oz*), and movie star Pearl White of *The Perils of Pauline*.

When he returned to England, his speaking schedule grew even more intense. The topics on which he talked make for a mind-boggling mix: "Spiritualism and the Child," "Liberty and Lunacy," "Truth and Tradition," "Higher and Lower Criticism," "Learning and Un-Learning," "The Cult of the Unreasonable," "The Perils of Plutocracy," "The Art of the Middle Ages," "The Use and Abuse of Hero Worship," "The Return of King Arthur," and of course he had to talk about his trip to America. Just as varied as the topics were the audiences to whom he spoke, from Oxford and Cambridge to women's social clubs to county fairs to local libraries to churches to the London School of Economics. At the Association of the Correctors of the Press, he said he came there to speak "as one whose writings invariably require a vast amount of correction."[63] He was the quintessential after-dinner speaker, boosting charitable events, charming audiences with his wit, capturing them with his wisdom, and cautioning them with his warnings about the way the world was going. One attendee observed:

> Public banquets, in the main, can be placed in two categories: either the dinner is good and the speeches unbearable, or the dinner and speeches alike are bad. However, I would eat the worst dinner in London if it afforded me the opportunity of listening to a speech by G. K. Chesterton.[64]

C. A. Dawson-Scott said that Chesterton's attitude contributed to his popularity. He was kind, but he was also courageous.

> He once asked me why he had unexpectedly been asked to speak at a certain public dinner which I had organized. He is, of course, a brilliant and amusing speaker, but that was not altogether the reason, and I did not quite dare to say, "Well, you see, you happen to be very much liked and people trust you."[65]

Asked to give a talk in honor of the Centennial of George MacDonald, Chesterton arrived late due to a heavy fog, but "improvised some delicious sentences out of his journey through the fog. He compared the light of Rationalism, which falls on things, with the light of mysticism, which shines through them, and he claimed George MacDonald as one of the truest mystics."[66] But he would occasionally leave his listeners in the fog, as he did the time he spoke at the Leeds Arts Club. A member of the club reminisced about that night many years later:

> At the appointed hour, he still had not arrived. Then, after several minutes, he burst in, mopping his brow, and had not given a thought to the subject of his lecture. "What shall I talk about?" he asked, looking about the room. Then a pause for inspiration. "Ah, yes," he said, "suppose I give you the reasons why a man should poison his grandmother?" A puzzled audience listened for about an hour while he, in true Chestertonian style, propounded his "reasons." And they left, as puzzled as ever.[67]

For the most part, however, he was dazzling. He once gave a talk arguing that his ideal of widespread property ownership was not a new idea but could be traced to medieval times. During the question period, a young lawyer by the name of Blanco White rose and challenged him on the point, saying there was absolutely no evidence for it and Chesterton had simply made it up. Chesterton calmly quoted a long passage from the Medieval Charter, *in the Old English*, to support his argument. Blanco White shrank back into his chair, "completely punctured."[68] The same thing once happened when an audience member claimed Chesterton's economic ideas contradicted Cardinal Newman. Chesterton laughed and said, "Oh, you won't catch me on Newman," and proceeded to quote Newman verbatim from memory in favor of what he had just said.[69]

He also engaged in dozens of debates with opponents of various renown including Shaw, but others as well: actresses, feminists, lawyers, scientists, Baptist preachers, cynical journalists, apoplectic politicians, smug university professors, and eager students. He pointed out the irony of being invited to participate in debates where the sponsoring group "expressed the earnest wish that nothing should be introduced that was at all controversial." He wondered "how we could most carefully ensure that there should be nothing controversial in a controversy." What was the most controversial subject? It was not politics. It was not even religion. It was money. "Anything criticizing the rich is controversial and anything justifying the rich is non-controversial."[70]

A young journalist named Beverley Nichols, who would go on to have a prolific career as a writer of novels, mysteries, and especially books on gardening, took on Chesterton in a debate about divorce. As with everyone who debated Chesterton, Nichols totally enjoyed both the experience and the opponent. He was amused by how Chesterton would laugh at his own jokes even before he had told them, chortling in anticipation of what he was about to say. But most interesting to Nichols was what Chesterton said after the debate was over:

> When we were standing in the hall, waiting for the car, he delivered of himself a second speech which so interested me that afterwards I went straight home to write it down.
>
> "Somebody said in the debate," he remarked, "that I am the slave of symbols, that I believed in magic, that in a ceremony or an institution or a faith I merely examined what was on the surface and took it all in like a peasant in the Middle Ages.
>
> "But it isn't I who is the slave of symbols. It is you. I venerate the idea which lies behind the symbol, you venerate only the empty shell. Take this case of monarchy. Somebody remarked tonight that we had

taken away half the duties and prerogatives of the King, and that the monarchy still remained. They went on to say that we could take away half the duties and prerogatives of marriage and that marriage would still remain. Perhaps it will, but what will be the use of it?

"Because I bow down before the sceptre, and because I take the words 'honour and obey' quite literally, you say that I am a slave of the symbol. But I bow down to the sceptre because I believe in the power that lies behind it. I keep to the smallest details of the marriage service because I believe in the marriage. If you believe in neither the sceptre or the marriage, and yet bow down to them, you are the slave of the symbol."

He looked away. Someone presented him with his macintosh. He struggled into it, got it half on, and then with one arm still waving in the air, he exclaimed:

"A time is coming—very soon—when you will find that you want this ideal of marriage. You will want it as something hard and solid to cling to in fast dissolving society. You will want it even more than you seem to want divorce today."[71]

Whenever he visited other countries, but especially when he visited his own, he would seek out small villages and countrysides where he would walk and draw and write and think and drink the local wine and eat the local cheese. He would amuse children by drawing pictures for them, usually pictures of two men sword-fighting, which would amuse them very much. He often got lost, which he greatly enjoyed doing and would provide fodder for a newspaper article. He especially enjoyed seaside towns, where he would walk along the stone walls or on the piers, watching the waves and contemplating the horizon.

Although he clearly enjoyed writing, it was still a chore. The basic nuisance of work "is not that the thing is intrinsically dull; it is that you want to do something else. My own present trade is more amusing than most, but I am cursing this article as fast as I write it, because I have an important appointment with myself on the top of a neighbouring hill that overlooks the flats towards the sea."[72]

And although critics have complained that the characters and action in his novels do not seem lifelike (Chesterton himself was among these critics), what few notice is that in many of his essays, when he gives accounts of things that have really happened to him in trains or in cafés or on the street, it reads like a page from a novel. If his art did not imitate life closely enough, his life always imitated art.

> ... a train came rather slowly into the station. It was an unnaturally dark train; I could not see a light anywhere in the long, black body of it; and I could not see any guard running beside it. I was reduced to walking up to the engine and calling out to the stoker to ask if the train was going to London. "Well—yes, sir," he said, with an unaccountable kind of reluctance. "It is going to London; but—." It was just starting, and I jumped into the first carriage: it was pitch-dark. I sat there smoking and wondering, as we steamed through the continually darkening landscape, lined with desolate poplars, until we slowed down and stopped, irrationally, in the middle of a field. I heard a heavy noise as of some one clambering off the train, and a dark, ragged head suddenly put itself into my window. "Excuse me, sir," said the stoker, "but I think, perhaps—well, perhaps you ought to know—there's a dead man in this train."[73]

In May of 1922, Chesterton had another encounter with death. His father Edward died at Gilbert's boyhood home in Kensington, after having been in declining health for several months. On his deathbed, he whispered to his son: "Even if I were to be a lost soul, life would have been worth living."[74]

Perhaps his father's death was the final piece in the puzzle. Or perhaps Gilbert was more like the weak-willed fellow in the Gospel who promised to follow Jesus as soon as he buried his father. "Let the dead bury the dead," came the rebuke. In any case, after Chesterton buried his father he wrote a letter to his mother informing her of his decision to become Catholic. In one sense, it was the culmination of his loyalty to his dead brother, who had converted a decade earlier. He explained to his mother that he was following in Cecil's footsteps. He wrote: "I am convinced that the fight for the family, for the free citizen and for everything that is decent must now be waged by the one fighting form of Christianity."[75] For G. K. Chesterton, it was always a battle, and he saw in the Catholic Church "the one fighting form of Christianity." A few weeks later Chesterton entered the Roman Catholic Church.

When the local vicar in Beaconsfield heard of Chesterton's conversion, he said that he was glad that Chesterton was becoming Catholic because "he had always been a very bad Anglican."[76]

He was certainly never much of a Protestant. He had long criticized Calvinism for the damage done by the doctrine of predestination, which had infected not only religion but secular philosophies from biology to economics to psychology, all of which exhibited different forms of determinism to the detriment of free will. He regarded the "Bible-worshippers" and the "Bible-smashers" as locked in a provincial quarrel in which they both miss the point (e.g., the Scopes Trial).[77] Though he was certainly familiar with Scripture, with plenty of biblical references seasoning his writing, the only book of the Bible he continually expounded on was the very unpopular (and misunderstood) Book of Job. The "cushioned chapels"[78] never seem to allow for suffering, which Chesterton saw as fundamental to the religious life, as Job's wounds prefigure those of Christ.[79] On the other hand, Puritanism is asceticism without joy. He saw that every Protestant sect has borrowed something from the Catholic Church and neglected the rest. Thus, each is indeed a "sect," or section of the whole Faith, something less, something representing division, and eventually decay.

As an Anglican, he had managed to regard himself as a Catholic until he finally could no longer escape the realization that the Church of England was also a Protestant sect. Ten years before his conversion, he said that every man is either moving toward or away from the Catholic Church. In the following decade he could see the direction in which whole Church of England was going. One of the most prominent Anglican clergymen of the day was the Reverend Doctor William Inge, who had been a professor of divinity at Cambridge and was a prolific writer, much-decorated with honorary degrees. He had recently been appointed to the prestigious and public position of dean of St. Paul's Cathedral. Inge had gained the epithet "The Gloomy Dean" after using his pulpit to deliver an over-the-top pessimistic lecture in 1920 entitled "The Idea of Progress," in which he lashed out at everything ever accomplished by Western Civilization and everything ever believed by those who went by the name of Christian. He was the prototypical "Broad Churchman" as opposed to "High Churchman." Tradition was bad, progress was good. Doctrine was bad because it divided people and was based on documents that were doubtful. He favored a more "spiritual" and "autonomous" form of Christianity, based on "experience and individual inspiration." He had no use for the common man whom Chesterton championed, and certainly not for the beliefs of the common man, which Chesterton affirmed. The dean dismissed "sacramentalism" because it was "obvious" that the lower classes were "natural idolaters" who believed in the Blessed Sacrament. In addition to throwing out the sacraments, he also threw out Scripture, that is, he embraced the "higher criticism," thereby emptying the Bible of any divinity. Thus, he rejected both "High Church" and "Low Church" Christians. Above all, he hated the Roman Catholic Church with "a raging hatred." He endorsed contraception and opposed organized labor, wringing his hands about "unwanted children" but once saying that strikers should be hanged. He was an outspoken eugenicist but also an early animal rights activist. The Gloomy Dean, it seems, is the person that Chesterton has in mind when he says, "Wherever you have animal worship, you will have human sacrifice."[80] In a characteristic twist, Chesterton calls him a master of paradox for his "being wrong on both sides at once." The Broad Churchmen like Dr. Inge, says Chesterton, "combine the widest cosmic doubts with the narrowest social sympathies. They will tell you blandly that they do not believe in the *vox populi vox dei*; but the truth is much more than that. The truth is that they would hate the *vox populi* much more if they thought it was the *vox dei*: for they fear all ultimate realities. That is what is meant by being broad-minded."[81]

Amazing to Chesterton is that so un-Christian a thinker could occupy such an important Christian post. The dean is, quite simply, a heathen.

> The Dean may be entitled, and doubtless he sincerely thinks himself entitled, to use the supreme pulpit of the supreme city of the British Empire to impose his individual shade of modernism or monism, or whatever it is that makes him doubt the resurrection of the body or the miracles of the New Testament. Still, our imagination can take in the possibility of a preacher

in the Apostle's Cathedral who should happen to be satisfied with the Apostles' Creed. We can call up the fancy picture of a priest of St. Paul's who should agree with St. Paul.[82]

Chesterton compares the Gloomy Dean to a Shakespearean fairy, "following darkness like a dream; that is, of moving from point to point so carefully as always to remain in the dark."[83] With a philosophy that leaves him in darkness, it makes sense that the dean is so gloomy. What makes no sense is that he is the dean.

While Chesterton's departure from the Church of England may not have bothered a growing progressive strain, other Anglicans were not so pleased to lose Chesterton. Conversions are generally not news, but Chesterton was a writer with "a world-wide circulation," and everyone agreed it was Rome's biggest catch since Cardinal Newman in the previous century. One prominent Anglican clergyman, Canon Headderly, said the Church of England lost its biggest intellectual asset in Chesterton, and that it was "on par with our general muddle-headedness as a religious body." He said the church never used Chesterton to its advantage, instead preferring "some dry-as-dust professor from Oxford to the sparkling paradox of the greatest wit of the century."[84]

What Canon Headderly had especially appreciated about Chesterton was that he "courteously and fairly" exploded the Puritan fallacies that had "taken away joy and beauty and love" from the faith "through sheer lack of humor." Chesterton had been "doing the work of angels who make merry in heaven."[85] And the Church of England bungled badly by not managing to keep him.

Similarly, an editorial in the Anglican weekly, the *Church Times*, said that what was strange about Chesterton was not that he had gone over to Rome, but that he had remained so long in the Anglican communion. It showed that growing liberalism was driving away the educated laity. Blasting the liberal Anglican bishop Hensley Henson, who encouraged doubt of the Virgin Birth and the Resurrection, the editor intoned: "Hensonism has never, we believe, attracted one educated man to the church; it has, we believe, robbed that church of the genius of G. K. Chesterton and of lesser men who are not content with cold negations."

The Catholic papers, not unexpectedly, sang a different tune. The *Tablet*'s headline crowed: "THE HOMECOMING OF MR. CHESTERTON." It also likened the conversion to that of Newman, and even repeated the very same words it had printed in 1845: "We congratulate him with most devoted affection on his happy conversion, and our readers in their share in the fortunate event. God knows it fills us with a joy we cannot adequately express." It especially expressed happiness over having Chesterton's happiness in the Church. "He will not let the devil have all the frolic."[86] Indeed, the Catholic papers, in anticipating what Chesterton would mean to the Church, hoped that he would not change with his conversion. They were looking for continuity. They wanted the same Chesterton they had already come to know; not a new one, just a Catholic one. They would get their wish.

When that local Anglican vicar said that Chesterton was never a very good Anglican, it may have been a reference to the fact that, as an Anglican, G. K. Chesterton hardly ever went to church. It is here where a true transformation took place. In that sense, GKC went from being a not very good Anglican to being a very good Catholic. After his conversion, he never missed a day of obligation. He said that only a religion that was true could get him out of bed so early in the morning. But there was no humor when it came to Communion. He approached the rail in fear and trembling. It affected him physically. Asked what was wrong, he responded: "I am afraid of that tremendous

Reality."[87] There is, says Chesterton, a "considerable practical difference between Jehovah pervading the universe and Jesus Christ coming into the room."[88]

In October of 1922, he granted his first interview about his conversion. The reporter was Henry Somerville, the London correspondent for the *Toronto Star*, who went to Beaconsfield to get the scoop more than two months after the fact. Chesterton told him it was the Protestants who helped convince him to become Catholic. He mentioned the Gloomy Dean and Bishop Henson: "Any church claiming to be an authoritative church must be quite definite when great questions of public morals are put forth. Can I go in for cannibalism or the murder of babies to reduce the population, or any other scientific or progressive reform? Any church with authority to teach must say whether it can be done. But the Protestant churches are in utter bewilderment on these moral questions: for example on birth control, on divorce . . . and one could mention other questions like suicide."[89] This is certainly on par with his earlier arguments in *Orthodoxy*, where he says that it was the opponents of Christianity who helped convince him that Christianity was true. It was now the opponents of the Catholic Church who helped convince him that it was the true Church.

He also found out, after becoming Catholic, that many people had been praying for his conversion, including his friend and fellow convert Maurice Baring, and all the nuns in a London convent.

A year later he spoke at the Roman Catholic Congress in Birmingham, England, as a guest of Cardinal Bourne. When introduced, GKC received a loud and sustained ovation. His announced topic: "The Catholic Church Does Not Die."

Though some were put off by his conversion, Chesterton's international reputation as a writer did not diminish.

In 1924 he was a guest at the PEN Luncheon in London, where the featured speaker was Czech playwright Karel Capek, who expressed his thanks to the English writers, including "your genial adventurer, Mr. Chesterton." The two had an "animated discussion" during the luncheon. Capek's most famous play, *R.U.R.*, gave us the term "robot," but interestingly, he got the idea from a Father Brown story, where the main suspects in a murder are the victim's "mechanical servants."

Chesterton traveled extensively for the last several years of his life, and though it was obviously enjoyable to see new places and meet new people, taking in the history and culture of foreign lands, travel was work and not leisure. Chesterton could easily have made enough money as a writer to support himself. But he supported others. In addition to putting nieces and nephews and godchildren through school, he had to support two newspapers: first the *New Witness* and then *G.K.'s Weekly*, paying staff members and printing bills. His speaking tours were one of the main sources of those needed funds. They were productive, no doubt fascinating, but also exhausting. Each year it was necessary that he and Frances take a two-week holiday, either to the southern coast of England, usually Brighton, or else to the western coast, usually Lyme-Regis. And for two weeks, every day, GKC would sit in a chair on the front porch of a hotel, all day long, surrounded by a pile of books and newspapers, and look out at the sea. "I never have enough nothing to do."[90] Like any other working man, he would stuff a year's worth of relaxation into a fortnight. It was while staying at Lyme-Regis that they met a widow and her daughters, the Nicholl family. They became such close friends that the Nicholls moved to Beaconsfield to be close to the Chestertons, living just a block away. Gilbert and Frances took an active interest in the lives of the Nicholl sisters, whom they treated as daughters, presenting them with gifts, including treasured original poems and stories and drawings at each of the major events in their lives.

One woman who grew up in Beaconsfield said that Chesterton always stood in the presence of a woman, no matter what her age or status, but he was especially deferential to little girls, treating them like queens. He never talked down to children. On the contrary, they always felt important around him and at ease. They called him "Mr. Tame Lion" or "Uncle Chestnut."

He was genuinely interested in what others had to say, but he had a weakness for answering questions with twenty-minute monologues, though no one complained. They sat enraptured while he spoke. He wore out the arms of chairs by thumping on them while he talked.

The locals loved him. He was once asked what he would do if he were elected magistrate. He answered, "Well, I suppose I would resign." This comment was put to the test one day when he arrived from London to discover that he had been elected town constable of Beaconsfield. The town officials paid a call to inform him of this honor. He told them that he could not fulfill the duties of a constable since one of those duties was to suppress local riots, and he was afraid he would be on the side of the rioters.

He was also appointed the official ale taster by the Lord Mayor of Beaconsfield, a purely honorary position that did not involve any actual duties, but naturally a legend arose that the local pubs objected to how much ale he entitled himself to taste. Chesterton enjoyed these jokes against himself. The other one he enjoyed repeating was when there was a loud construction project on the lot next to Top Meadow, and his neighbors went and complained to the foreman, "Mr. Chesterton can't write!" who had the prized comeback: "Yes. We're aware of that."[91]

The local residents' appreciation and admiration of him revealed itself in large ways and small. His gardener used to pick up Chesterton's cigar butts and smoke the remnant in his pipe. It was not because he was being thrifty; it was a way of showing reverence.

Chesterton would stroll to the local pubs, the White Hart and the Saracen's Head, in order to have convivial conversations with the local residents, to find out what they were thinking about the issues of the day. He defended the common man not from lofty heights and a remote study, but from the perspective of sitting side-by-side with him at the table or at the bar. The other regular destination was the town barber, where the locals always enjoyed his great talk. One day he arrived for his haircut, and a little boy was waiting in line before him. Gilbert was in a hurry and offered the boy a coin if he could cut in front of him. The boy was only too happy to oblige the famous town resident. The next time Chesterton came in for his haircut, there were *two* little boys who just happened to be there waiting in line. GKC smiled and gave them both a tip for passing privileges. This occurrence continued on a regular basis and the line grew each time, till it became a ritual, Chesterton laughing as he handed out money to a long line of little boys on his way to the barber's chair. When the barbershop was renovated many years after Chesterton's death, the proprietors could not bring themselves to throw away the chair that Chesterton sat in. It was an honored throne. So it was presented as a gift to the Chesterton Study Centre in honor of its most esteemed occupant and tribute to his generosity toward the common man who came to hear him speak from the chair . . . and the little boys who came and stood in line ahead of him.

In the spring of 1926, he went to Spain on a speaking tour. The Queen of Spain attended his talk in Madrid. He was feted in Barcelona and throughout Catalonia. In the seaside town of Sitges, the local citizens erected a bronze monument with a relief sculpture of Chesterton in recognition of his poem *Lepanto*. The monument still stands.

On All Saints Day of that year, Gilbert received one of his greatest gifts, one that he had patiently hoped for but could hardly expect. After four long years, his wife Frances finally joined him in the Catholic Church. When asked what made her become Catholic, she replied, "The devil." She had taken instruction on her own and was received by the Bishop of Northampton. That strange and uncomfortable divide between her and her husband was bridged, then and forever. After death, resurrection. Like his conversion, hers also represented a kind of continuity rather than a dramatic transition. Her embrace of the Church was complete, and she proceeded with ease and grace as if she had always been Catholic. She was soon teaching Sunday School. But the visits to the Catholic countries became all the more meaningful, beginning with a trip to Poland six months later.

In Poland, Gilbert and Frances received the most royal treatment they ever had in their lives. They were greeted by large, cheering crowds at each city where their train arrived. In Warsaw, they were actually escorted from the station by the Polish Cavalry in glittering full dress. Chesterton had always been a defender of Poland as "the pillar of Europe," and he was welcomed as a champion in every respect. Frances reported how the speeches of their hosts were delivered in "quite colloquial and very witty" English, showing "a detailed knowledge" of Chesterton's works far surpassing that of any of her English acquaintances. Gilbert's own speeches were deeply appreciated. He gave a very moving address to the PEN Club, reducing the audience to tears. Dorothy Collins said she had never heard a more inspiring talk. He was taken all around the country, including some villages on the Soviet border. He met princes and peasants and learned firsthand of their suffering and perseverance as Poland had been used as a pawn in world events over the previous decades. The same thing would happen again in the following decades. Amazingly, Chesterton never wrote a book about Poland, though the country and its people were never far from his thoughts. It was one of the many planned volumes from his vast unwritten library, which he said would also include books about the places he had never been.

He returned from Poland with a new walking stick that was hand-carved on the mountain of Zakopane. Its handle consisted of an eagle's head on one side and a battle-ax on the other. It became his favorite for the rest of his life, appearing in almost every photograph of him taken thereafter.

In October of 1929, he traveled to Rome where he had private audiences with two of the most famous people in the world: Benito Mussolini and Pope Pius XI. Though Mussolini's reputation has since acquired a heavy layer of tarnish, at the time he was not just the ruler of Italy but an international celebrity whose every move was news. Although Chesterton admired him for the way he rebuilt war-torn Italy by appealing to its rich history and tradition, he was very skeptical of Fascism. Chesterton's critics claimed then (and some still do) that Chesterton supported Fascism, but he flatly informed them that they were "under a misapprehension."[92] He preferred democracy to dictatorship and local government to centralized government. He said that describing Fascism is not the same as endorsing it. He described it thus: "Fascism has brought order into the State; but this will not be lasting, unless it has brought back order into the Mind."[93] He speculated that it was very possible there would be a war with Mussolini's Italy because something about it was askew. "It may some day be necessary to fight the new force of the Mediterranean."[94] Chesterton was always a critic of the British Fascists, and was especially critical of their anti-Semitism. To make things confusing, he had a distant cousin who was a member of the British Fascists, and he had similar initials: A. K., as opposed to G. K. It is very possible that G. K. Chesterton's unfortunate and undeserved reputation as an anti-Semite is due to things said by A. K. Chesterton.

As for G. K.'s meeting with Mussolini, the two of them agreed to speak in French to each other. Chesterton said, "My French is better than my Italian," and Mussolini responded, "And my French is better than your French." Ironically, the main topic of their conversation was the status of the Church of England. Apparently, Mussolini felt uncomfortable talking about the Catholic Church. But it did not prevent him from doing almost all the talking while Chesterton did very little.

Chesterton also did not talk much when he met the Pope, but for a very different reason. The master of words was at a loss for words:

> I found in the presence of the Pope that I could not talk English, or talk at all. He came suddenly out of his study, a sturdy figure in a cape, with a square face and spectacles, and began speaking to me about what I had written, saying some very generous things about a sketch I wrote of St. Francis of Assisi. He asked me if I wrote a great deal; and I answered in fragmentary French phrases that it was only too true, or words to that effect. The clerical dignitary nobly struck in in my support by saying it was my modesty. As a matter of fact, my head was in a whirl and it might have been anything. Then he made a motion and we all knelt; and in the words that followed I understood for the first time something that was once meant by the ceremonial use of the plural; and in a flash I saw the sense of something that had always seemed to me a senseless custom of kings. With a new strong voice, that was hardly even like his own, he began *Nous vous benissons*, and I knew that something stood there infinitely greater than an individual; I knew that it

was indeed *We*; We, Peter and Gregory and Hildebrand and all the dynasty that does not die.[95]

When the audience was ended and he made his way out of the papal palace, past the Swiss guards, and into the open air of St. Peter's Square, he said to his host, "That frightened me more than anything I have known in my life."[96] He was unable to work or concentrate for several days.

He saw the Pope two more times during the trip, but in less intimate settings: first while with a group of English pilgrims who had come to attend the Beatification of the English Martyrs, and then at the beatification itself, where thousands of people were present. He said the great pageantry meant much to him, that it was indeed a powerful emotional experience, as was everything in Rome among the soaring and inspiring ecclesial architecture.

> ... yet I do not base my belief on such emotions, still less on such pageants or shows. I was myself received into the Catholic Church in a small tin shed, painted brick-red, which stood among the sculleries and outhouses of a Railway Hotel. That represents with great exactitude the precise extent to which I was or am influenced by exquisite architecture or alluring music or storied windows richly dight, casting a dim religious light. And the Pope would be the first to say that the step I took in entering that shed was inconceivably more important than the step of entering St. Peter's, or the Vatican, or his own presence.[97]

Chesterton's inability to speak in the presence of the Pope epitomized his entire experience in Rome. His great powers of language utterly failed him in trying to describe the Eternal City. But that did not stop him from writing a book about it. He said he could have written an entire book merely by looking out of the window of his hotel room. Indeed, he had one of the best views of the entire city from the Hotel Hassler at the top of the Spanish Steps. His problem, however, was wanting to write about everything. And Rome simply provides too much material. "Rome," he said, "is too small for its greatness, or too great for its smallness."[98]

He and Frances stayed in Rome for two months, with side trips to Assisi and other cities. He gave several lectures, including a talk on Blessed Thomas More, sponsored by the Roma Unitas Society. It was "attended by one of the most distinguished audiences Rome can muster."[99] There was a great demand for entry cards, and hundreds were turned away.

In 1930 Chesterton was elected the first president of the Detection Club, a group of mystery writers who met at a London restaurant in a private room to discuss their craft. There was a tongue-in-cheek secret ritual involving a crystal skull, and a code of conduct to which all of them agreed. It involved being fair to the reader and avoiding hackneyed tricks of the trade. Ghosts were not allowed to be murderers. Neither were identical twins. It was a combination of good fun but also a sense of honor. Members included Agatha Christie, Ronald Knox, Dorothy L. Sayers, and A. A. Milne (more famous as the creator of Winnie the Pooh.) Who wasn't a member? Arthur Conan Doyle. He was more interested in his Spiritualism than he was in his fictional detective, Sherlock Holmes.

In October of that year, there was a big event on the campus of the University of Notre Dame in Indiana. It was the opening of the new football stadium. Knute Rockne gave a speech. A Navy admiral gave a speech. The president of Notre Dame, Fr. Charles O'Donnell, gave a speech and told the emotional story about George Gipp's last game. And then a special guest was introduced and there was a loud and uproarious standing ovation for him. It was G. K. Chesterton, who had just arrived from England and had never seen a football game in his life.

According to the report, thousands of "lusty voices shouted the name of one of the world's leading literary lights." Everyone at the university considered it a good omen.

For the first time in his life, Chesterton had been invited to be a visiting professor. For the next six weeks he gave eighteen lectures on Victorian literature and the same number on Victorian history and politics.

At least five hundred students attended each lecture, but Emil Telfil, editor of the school paper, lamented that the hall should have been full to capacity (which, if the balcony were stuffed, would have been almost nine hundred). He complained about the "warped sense of values" on campus, which was always in a fever about football and "distinctly secondary college activities" while "very little thought is given to things intellectual and cultural." He said that the students were not taking full advantage of Chesterton's presence on campus, and by the time they realize what they have missed "there [would] not be another great mind to listen to."

Nonetheless, those who attended were held spellbound night after night. Chesterton would ascend the stage every evening, digging through his pockets, looking for his notes, and finally produce a scrap of paper, from which he would lecture for about an hour. It turns out there was almost nothing written on these supposed notes. "What I like about notes," he would later say, "is that once you begin you can completely disregard them."[100]

The only record we have of these lectures is from the notebooks of three students, which are preserved in the University Archives. Here are a few sound bites gleaned from them:[101]

> On Mary Queen of Scots: "She was executed for being in good health."

On Thomas Carlyle: "His beliefs were all make-beliefs."

On Edward Bulwer-Lytton (he of the "It was a dark and stormy night" fame): "He was quite successfully modern which is the reason why he is almost forgotten."

On George Eliot: "She was not a hilarious person."

On Thackeray: "His greatest cynicism is on cynicism."

On Matthew Arnold: "He was fanatical against fanaticism."

On Robert Browning: "He could pass quickly from the ridiculous to the sublime without seeming ridiculous."

On Oscar Wilde: "He worshipped beauty to the neglect of truth and morality. As a result, poetry became artificial."

On George Bernard Shaw and H. G. Wells: "They tried to fulfill Victorian ideals which were never meant to be fulfilled."

"Poetry is the flower of civilization," said Chesterton in one lecture. "Romanticism has worked itself out in our time in nonsense and dirt. We should remind the humanists that if poetry has become too personal it has also become unpoetic." Chesterton was no mere critic of the poets he criticized; he also knew how to appreciate them, reciting long passages of their poetry from memory. One evening, he recited three hundred lines of Swinburne. His command of the subject matter astonished everyone.

His lectures included nothing about modern poetry. But one young professor, Rufus William Rauch, would bring a few students with him to the home where Chesterton was staying to discuss modern poetry. He asked if the distinguished man of letters was familiar with T.S. Eliot. Chesterton proceeded to quote the long opening passage from *Ash Wednesday,* which had just been published in the *Criterion.* Then he mused reflectively, "Quite dizzying. I suppose that's one way to conversion." Rauch was amazed—at that moment and ever after.

The guest lecturer graced the university with a poem of his own. It was entitled *The Arena,* and in it, he contrasted the gladiators of old with the present day Catholic football players: "Youth untroubled; youth untortured; hateless war and harmless mirth," who partake of "a holier bread" in "a happier circus" and who hail their Queen with a glorious (as opposed to gory) cry of "We who are about to *live* salute thee!" One professor said it was the most mystical approach to football ever taken.

Despite his demanding schedule, it was not all work and no play for the Englishman visiting South Bend. Prohibition was still in effect, and so he insisted on being taken to a speakeasy. He also observed that Prohibition wasn't all bad since many Notre Dame professors had shown a lot of resourcefulness and ingenuity, building stills in their basements and also brewing their own beer. He suggested that perhaps everything should be prohibited, which would make people more self-sufficient.

There was a notable change of attitude toward Chesterton from his visit to America ten years earlier. He had gone from being merely famous to being "distinguished." And his attitude toward America won him over especially to the staid Midwesterners. Sinclair Lewis had just been awarded the Nobel Prize for Literature, and Chesterton said he was not the best American literary representative. He said Thornton Wilder or Edith Wharton would have been better choices because Lewis belittled the typical American and mocked Main Street. Chesterton exalted the common man and defended Main Street. The Americans took note of the contrast between Lewis and Chesterton; it was the difference between an alienated insider and a sympathetic outsider. In South Bend, Chesterton had stayed for six weeks in a typical middle-class home, "an ordinary, jolly little frame house," and found it utterly charming, wholesome, and egalitarian. One American editor admitted, "Maybe the real Main Street that most of us live on isn't so bad, after all."[102] More somberly, another editor admitted that "the clear-eyed Chesterton" had come along as a counterpoint to the American confidence in the machine age, and he quoted him approvingly: "We have given ourselves over to an insatiable monster who serves us at the price of our slavery."[103]

At the end of his stay at Notre Dame, Chesterton was given an honorary doctorate by Fr. O'Donnell, and the event was national news.

GK and Frances had an emotional parting with the Bixler family at whose home they had stayed, and then embarked on a strenuous lecture tour of America that lasted several months into the following year, taking them coast-to-coast. In January of 1931, Chesterton debated Clarence Darrow at the Mecca Hall in New York City. Four thousand people attended and voted 3-to-1 that Chesterton had won the debate. One reporter complained that it had been billed as the Clash of the Titans, but only one Titan showed up. Darrow thought he could do Scopes all over again but found a superior debater and a superior thinker in Chesterton, who demolished him. One observer said that Chesterton wasn't even getting his exercise with Darrow, whose arguments were "positively muddle-headed." Historians tend to overlook the fact that the great agnostic who made William Jennings Bryan look so foolish at the Scopes Trial six years earlier was himself made to look ridiculous by Chesterton in front of a much larger audience than could fill a small courtroom. Two of the three main Darrow biographies make no mention of the Chesterton debate. When religion wins the day, it goes unnoticed and unreported. That's because the normal is never news.[104]

When traveling through Tennessee, ironically the site of the Scopes Trial, Frances became so ill that she had to check into a hospital in Chattanooga. Their secretary, Dorothy Collins, stayed with her, while Gilbert was forced to travel alone to several cities before returning to Tennessee, where Frances was slowly recovering. Gilbert arrived back in Chattanooga in a total mess, having slept in his clothes for several days and cleaned his nails rather ineffectively with a pencil. How he made it to his lectures and caught any of the right trains remains a mystery if not a miracle. A few subsequent lectures had to be canceled while Frances continued to convalesce, before they made their way to California.

Chesterton recycled a few of his lecture titles from his previous trip to America, since he was working a new audience, but he added some new ones as well, including "The Age of Unreason," "The Curse of Psychology," and "Culture and the Coming Peril." We learn from a published transcript of the last speech what the coming peril is: "To put it shortly, the evil I am trying to warn you of is not excessive democracy, it is not excessive ugliness, it is not excessive anarchy. It might be stated thus: It is standardization by a low standard."[105]

After Chesterton's speech in Oakland, California, the archbishop of San Francisco, E. J. Hanna, stood and said to the audience: "You have listened to one of the world's wisest men."[106]

A Seattle reporter described the spectacle of Chesterton's arrival:

> Completely enveloped in a huge black cape that looked as if it might have been handed down from old Doctor Johnson himself, with a few reminiscent crumbs from the taverns of old London still clinging to its folds, Gilbert K. Chesterton came to town yesterday.
>
> The great man of English letters sat in the aisle of the parlor car of the Vancouver train, posing for a

photographer, his eyes peering merrily over and under and around, but never through an antiquated pair of spectacles, the like of which have never been seen in these parts before.

Chesterton is never mistaken for anyone else. His whimsical though distinctive mode of dress is a continual source of amusement to his literary contemporaries and friends, who frequently picture him as a great mountain of a man weighed down with clothing, the last stand of an old school against the invasion of modernity.[107]

In Los Angeles, Dorothy Collins met with some film producers and tried to negotiate some deals for the screen rights to the Father Brown stories and Chesterton's play *Magic*, but to no avail. The stay in southern California, however, was of great benefit, as the weather was especially salubrious to Frances. On their return cross-country trip, they saw the Grand Canyon, about which Chesterton wrote nothing. Neither did he mention the Pacific Ocean, the Rocky Mountains, or the mighty redwoods. But he talked about small towns, ugly architecture, and friendly people. They departed from New York in mid-April. The money raised from his many lectures on the seven-month trip all went into *G. K.'s Weekly*. The bulk of it came from Notre Dame.

The following year, 1932, he was a special guest at the International Eucharistic Conference in Dublin, where he was again welcomed to Ireland with exceeding warmth. The general sentiment in Ireland was that Chesterton, always a friend to the Irish, was actually the Irishman and Shaw was actually the Englishman. The Irish Friends of Chesterton donated the church bell for the bell tower in St. Teresa's Catholic Church in Beaconsfield in Chesterton's memory.

This was also the year that GKC began an entirely new venture. He became a regular presence on the radio. He was invited by BBC Radio to give bi-weekly broadcasts of book reviews. It was an opportunity for many people to hear his voice for the first time. Thousands bought radios just to hear Chesterton speak every two weeks.[108] His first broadcast was on October 31, 1932. The following day, the *Manchester Guardian* reported, "Mr. Chesterton's manner at the microphone is pleasant, the voice deep and slow, and all the time a conversational tone. It is one of those voices that will soon become a familiar one on the wireless—once heard, not easily forgotten."[109] Chesterton changed the nature of radio broadcasting by making it more intimate, speaking in a conversational tone, rather than in the typical shouting voice of an announcer. He achieved this by having Frances or Dorothy sit across from him while he spoke into the microphone, and he spoke to them rather than to the invisible audience. The fact that his voice is characterized as being deep contrasts with the many reports of those who heard him speak in person as saying that his voice was surprisingly high-pitched. There are a few extant recordings of his voice, and what strikes the listener is that it is of a normal pitch, neither high nor low. It seems that people who saw or met Chesterton were expecting a large low voice to come from the large man. A normal voice seemed too small and too high.

In February of 1933, his mother, Marie Louise Chesterton, died peacefully at the home where Chesterton had grown up. Upon her death, GKC inherited the bulk of her estate and for the first time in his life was financially secure. Although his mother had never enjoyed an especially warm relationship with her daughter-in-law, she credited Frances for keeping Gilbert out of debt. She was buried in the same grave as her husband and daughter in nearby Brompton Cemetery. Cecil's name is also carved on the tombstone though he is buried in a military cemetery in France.

A few weeks after Marie Chesterton was laid to rest, Dorothy Collins was horrified to find Chesterton at his parents' home throwing away all his father's papers. Edward had carefully preserved everything ever written by or about GKC from his childhood onward—manuscripts, notebooks, drawings, pamphlets, clippings, and more. Gilbert had two huge loads hauled away before his secretary arrived to stop him. For the Chesterton scholar, the event is nearly like unto the burning of the Library of Alexandria. He made it difficult on the students who would study him. He honestly considered his own work to be rubbish. He was also very likely overwhelmed by the sheer volume of it. Everyone else was. But that day was a great loss for the rest of us. What was saved, however, is still a mountain of material, several lifetimes' worth of reading and research. After being stored for years in the attic of Dorothy Collins's home, at least it is now relatively safe in the British Library. When the representative from the British Library came to collect it, she said, "There is more here than one person could have possibly written." And that was after who knows how much had been destroyed. Chesterton simply was not impressed with his own literary accomplishments. Once when asked to sign a complete set of his published books for a special presentation to an important admirer, he looked at the pile of volumes and said he felt like a man suddenly confronted by all his past crimes. He enjoyed reciting other people's poetry but never his own, and hearing his own works read aloud was absolute torture for him. On one occasion he was asked to recite his own poems and he said he could not remember any of them. Someone else stood up and said "I can" and proceeded to recite several of Chesterton's poems, including all of *Lepanto*. It was the poet Alfred Noyes, author of "The Highwayman."

In May of 1934, the Vatican announced that Chesterton had been made a Knight of the Order of St. Gregory by

Pope Pius XI. Often depicted as a knight both in caricature and in print, now Chesterton really was one. But he never made any reference to this great honor in any of his writings. England never honored him with a knighthood, as it did other important writers.

In 1935, Chesterton again traveled through Spain, France, and Italy. The main destination was Florence, where he gave an important and scholarly address on English Literature and the Latin Tradition. The speech was in honor of Luigi Pirandello, who had been awarded the Nobel Prize in Literature the year before and was most famous for his play *Six Characters in Search of an Author*. Ironically, and unknown to anyone but a few friends, Chesterton had just written a play in which, he said, he would "out-Pirandello Pirandello." The play was *The Surprise* and is considered by many to be his best play, but it was never performed during his lifetime. Even more ironically, it was at this time that Torsten Fogelqvist of the Swedish Academy nominated Chesterton for the Nobel Prize in Literature in 1935, the year after Pirandello had won. But Chesterton would not win. The papers of the Nobel committee, made public almost sixty years later, reveal the reason why Chesterton didn't win. As explained by Judge Per Hallström:

> The expert report willingly and cordially recognizes the genius of this writer, but has decided to recommend the rejection of the proposal, due to Chesterton's many eccentricities. His preaching is of high value and his critical acumen is almost unique, yet on the other hand he has acquired a very heavy load of frantically nervous, rash and absurd judgments and views. As an educator in a time in which nobody like Chesterton has realized the tentative helplessness of all essentials, his writings still cannot be considered helpful. A Nobel

Prize for Mr. Chesterton would only be justified as an admiration of his eminent intelligence, not of the effect of that same intelligence.[110]

Apparently Chesterton's intelligence had little effect. And who was it who beat out Chesterton that year? Nobody. The committee did not give anyone the Prize. Perhaps if he had just stuck to poetry, he would have won it. Great poets tend to be admired for their poetry without being taken to task for their philosophy.

Five years earlier, GKC had been overlooked for another honor. He was attending the Royal Literary Fund dinner when it was announced that John Masefield had been named Poet Laureate. Masefield was certainly a well-regarded poet who had published his share of poetry, including a very moving ballad, *The Everlasting Mercy*. But he was primarily known (and still is) for one poem: "Sea Fever." There was a general dissatisfaction with the news, but Chesterton, ever gracious, said: "He is an extremely fine poet, and I am very glad to hear it. I hope he will go on writing poems about drunken pirates."[111] In anticipation of the announcement, literary critic Patrick Braybrooke had said earlier, "Chesterton deserves to be Poet Laureate and fortunately never will be." It is perhaps a dubious distinction if not a curse. Masefield never wrote anything noteworthy again, but always felt obligated to do so, whereas even Chesterton's obligatory poems were spontaneous. He was an absolute natural. He could produce a poem as quickly as a pun, reeling off ballades, triolets, and clerihews with utter spontaneity. Words were his craft but also his playthings.

Interestingly, Chesterton made the Royal Literary Fund the beneficiary of his book royalties after his death. His home went to the Catholic Church to be used by the Convert Aid Society, giving housing to Anglican clergy who converted to

Catholicism—and who subsequently lost their jobs and homes. Top Meadow was put to active use for about four decades, but was shuttered up in the 1980s and eventually sold to a private party in the 1990s. Ironically, had the Convert Aid Society, now called the St. Bartholomew Society, hung onto it a little longer, it could be put back to use according to Chesterton's desired wishes, as there has been a flurry of conversions in recent years due to the Ordinariate established by Pope Benedict XVI, and also due to Anglican clergy's reading G. K. Chesterton. At least the property is protected as a historically designated building. It is well-preserved and worth a lot more than the Church sold it for.

In May of 1936, Chesterton took another trip to France and purposely included a pilgrimage to Lourdes. (No one goes to Lourdes as a mere tourist.) He was hoping for something from the healing waters there. He knew he was dying. Perhaps that is why he had completed his autobiography a month earlier.

Here's another date: June 14, 1936.

GKC had been in his bed for about three days, drifting in and out of consciousness. He was suffering from congestive heart failure. The day before the local priest, Monsignor Smith, had given him the Last Rites. Fr. Vincent McNabb, the Dominican priest whom Chesterton called the greatest man in England, had also visited. He sung the *Salve Regina* over Gilbert, then picked up the pen on the bedside table and kissed it. And he called G. K. Chesterton the greatest man in England.

At one point, the dying man opened his eyes and said, "The issue is now quite clear. It is between light and darkness and every one must choose his side."[112]

Many years earlier, near the very beginning of his career, he had written:

> We all wake up on a battlefield. We see certain
> squadrons in certain uniforms gallop past; we take an

arbitrary fancy to this or that colour, to this or that plume. But it often takes us a long time to realise what the fight is about or even who is fighting whom. . . . So in the modern intellectual world we can see flags of many colours, deeds of manifold interest; the one thing we cannot see is the map. We cannot see the simplified statement which tells us what is the origin of all the trouble. How shall we manage to state in an obvious and alphabetical manner the ultimate query, the primordial pivot on which the whole modern problem turns? It cannot be done in long rationalistic words; they convey by their very sound the suggestion of something subtle. One must try to think of something in the way of a plain street metaphor or an obvious analogy. For the thing is not too hard for human speech; it is actually too obvious for human speech.[113]

The thing too hard for human speech, the thing too obvious for human speech, was the thing G. K. Chesterton was always trying to say. He tried to bring clarity to all the confusion, tried to bring truth to a world of falsehood and deception. It was always a battle. Now, on this day, on a sunny June morning, Gilbert Keith Chesterton died on the battlefield where he had first found himself. He had chosen his side. He had fought against the darkness on behalf of the light.

Three days later the streets of Beaconsfield were lined with mourners. The funeral carriage had to be rerouted so that more people could bid farewell to the town's most beloved resident. The funeral was attended by personalities as diverse as Aldous Huxley and Fulton Sheen. After the funeral Hilaire Belloc was found at the White Hart, the famous local pub, crying uncontrollably. No one could accept it. Gilbert was gone. The newly-widowed Frances uttered the painful and pitiful words, "I can't believe he doesn't need me anymore."

He was buried in the tiny Roman Catholic cemetery in Beaconsfield. Ten days later, in London, Westminster Cathedral was filled for a Requiem Mass. Fr. O'Connor presided. The Archbishop read a telegram written by the Papal Secretary of State on behalf of Pope Pius XI expressing the Holy Father's grief at the loss of Chesterton, whom he called "a gifted defender of the faith." The British press would not print it because the term "Defender of the Faith" is reserved for the King of England. The author of the telegram, Cardinal Eugenio Pacelli, would himself become Pope Pius XII three years later.

Monsignor Ronald Knox, who credited his own conversion in part to having read G. K. Chesterton, *before Chesterton himself converted*, stood in the pulpit and praised the man who was loved by so many around the world. He imagined Chesterton being escorted into Heaven by St. Francis of Assisi and St. Thomas Aquinas, the two saints he wrote about.

"With me," Francis would say, "he loved the poor."

"With me," Thomas would say, "he loved the truth."

Novelist and poet Walter de la Mare penned the poetic tribute for the memorial card:

Knight of the Holy Ghost, he goes his way,
Wisdom his motley, Truth his loving jest;
The mills of Satan keep his lance in play,
Pity and Innocence his heart at rest.

From beginning to end, Chesterton was characterized as a knight. In the farewell poem, he is portrayed as still at battle, still going his way, still paradoxical, for his fool's attire is actually wisdom, his joke is actually the truth, and the fight is a delight. The devil doesn't get the joke. The dragon can't be taken seriously. The knight, ever of good humor, is at peace, his heart at rest because it is compassionate and pure. And, even today, he is still lovable, which is why people still love him. Still truthful, which is why he is still controversial.

Knight of the Holy Ghost, he goes his way. One of his earliest books was *The Wild Knight*, and he will always be associated with its title character, who says: "I ride forever, seeking after God."

THE WRITER

"I think the artist is the man who ought to be able to say what everybody else means."[1]

There are two theories about the amount of Chesterton's writing, both of which cast him in a negative light, but for opposite reasons. One is that he wrote too much. The other is that because he took such poor care of himself and died at only sixty-two years of age, he robbed the world of more of his writing. The first idea, I suppose, is that his quality suffered from his quantity, which was his own fault; and the second is that his quantity suffered from the poor quality of his health, which was his own fault. Both imply that in spite of the fact that G. K. Chesterton, who wrote more than just about anyone who ever lived, writing right up until his death, didn't do enough. He neglected his talent. He was somehow inadequate. The critics recognize Chesterton's enormous talent but they manage to complain about it. They say that he wrote too much but also that he was a master without a masterpiece, that his multiplicity of output somehow diluted the product. While discussing another author who was guilty of the same wide-ranging talent and gigantic achievement, Chesterton addressed the same criticism: "It is like complaining that a really good ale-house provides too much ale; which would seem not only a blasphemy but almost a contradiction in terms. It is like complaining that a really good popular singer can sing too many different songs; a complaint that is entirely a compliment."[2]

The problem is not that Chesterton is inadequate but that the theories about him are. He is simply too big to get a hold of. Too big to be seen. The critics cannot approach him because they are overwhelmed. So they choose to focus on something small and piddly, and make a fuss about it, and thereby consign this great writer to the dustbin. But though they have largely succeeded in keeping Chesterton out of the classroom, they have not succeeded in keeping him out of print.

Over seventy of his one hundred books have been republished. Essentially all of his poetry is available—over 1,500 pages—for the first time. But his books and his poetry represent only a fraction of his writing. He was primarily a journalist, and he wrote over 5,000 essays for newspapers and magazines. Over half of these have been collected into printed volumes. And then there are his ever-popular Father Brown stories, which have never gone out of print, and have continued to find new life on the screen.

To survey all of this writing in one chapter would be foolhardy and impossible, so that is what we are going to do. It is useless to look at a writer's life without looking at his writing. That is where we best see him, and see him at his best. That is where we will look now, first at his books, then his poetry, his journalism, and his Father Brown stories.

Chesterton's Books

Chesterton wrote a hundred books. Some, admittedly, are edited collections of previously published essays, some are merely extended pamphlets, and some are wartime propaganda that hold little interest today. But his novels continue to draw attention, and his religious and philosophical works only grow in stature.

We will consider five of his most important books: *Orthodoxy, What's Wrong with the World, St. Francis of Assisi, St. Thomas Aquinas,* and *The Everlasting Man.* This means leaving out some of his other most important books, such as his unsurpassable masterwork *Charles Dickens,* his prophetic tome *Eugenics and Other Evils,* his essential treatise *The Outline of Sanity,* his memorable book on the now forgotten painter G.F. Watts, and all his novels.

Orthodoxy

There is no other book like *Orthodoxy.* It doesn't compare with anything, which is what makes it so much like Chesterton's other books. In it, he tries to do what he always tries to do: explain sanity. But he is hampered by having to write for an insane world. Thus, he comes off as somewhat paradoxical. The obvious thing is the hardest to see. How would you, for instance, defend civilization when asked? Where do you begin? You might point to a chair or a piano. Anything that separates us from savagery. But there's still a lot of explaining to do. Similarly, how does the Christian defend Christianity? Especially to people who think they already understand it enough to dismiss it? That is the quest given to the knight in this tale. Chesterton claims it is not a book of apologetics. But, of course, it is. Everything in it defends his faith, just like everything else he writes.

Normally the place to begin when talking about God is the fact that we do not have a very good relationship with God. Something about sin and separation. But in the modern world, sin is not a subject that can be discussed at all. Though Chesterton says it is the only Christian doctrine that can actually be proved, it is outright denied. We cannot talk about God because we cannot talk about our broken relationship with God.

So Chesterton takes a different approach. He considers the various philosophies that have visited the world over the last few centuries. He concludes, in short order, that if we take any of them to their logical conclusion, we would end in a padded cell. But it gets worse. The modern philosophies are not only barking mad, they are self-destructive. He then compares them with the thing they all attack. What they attack is Christianity, but they attack it for opposite reasons. They contradict each other so that they might contradict Christianity. They would destroy the world so that they might destroy the Church. In the end, it is the Church that is left standing, and everything else is sprawling. In the end, the heresies lie prostrate, the "wild truth, reeling but erect."[3]

But where do we first find the truth? In the place where we first find anything—in the nursery. Fairy tales are the most elemental way that eternal verities are passed from one generation to the next. We learn that we will need courage and humility and charity in order to accomplish any great task. All the things a good and gentle, and a heroic, knight needs. We see in the fairy tale that all virtue is an "if." We will be happy if we follow a rule. We will be miserable if we break the rule. So will everyone else. The one who breaks the rules ruins the game for everyone.

Very subtly, we move to the topic of sin after all, but more importantly we come to redemption. We find a God that even the atheists can bear, for at one moment even he cried their cry of abandonment. He cried it from the Cross. Never has a defense of Christ been so unexpected, never so unorthodox as in *Orthodoxy*. Every sentence in this book is packed tight. Unpacking each is like unwrapping a gift, the best kind of gift—a surprise gift.

The Bible tells us plainly that "Jesus wept." But Chesterton reveals the great hidden truth implied in the rest of the Gospel story, the good news that seems too good to be told—Jesus laughed.

What's Wrong with the World

This is the book that launched what would become one of the main themes of his writing, as well as one of the main missions of his life. Though he does not begin to propound on the solution, he explains here the problem, or what's wrong with the world. He says there are four main things wrong with the world: big government, big business, feminism, and public education. The pain of this list, compiled in 1910, remains spectacular. Why are these the things that are wrong with the world? Because they all undermine the family, which is the basic unit of society, the thing that must be stable for society to be stable, the thing that must be strong for society to be strong, and the thing that is most under attack in our society today.

Big business, which Chesterton calls Gudge, wishes to break up the family. Big government, which Chesterton calls Hudge, wishes to replace the functions of the family. Gudge has already pulled the father out of the home, separating him from his family all day, but it has successfully pulled the mother out of the home as well, using feminism as its tool. Chesterton says pithily, "Ten thousand women marched through the streets saying, 'We will not be dictated to!' and went off and became stenographers."[4] In the meantime, Gudge does not have to pay a living wage to a father, when he can get two workers, father and mother, at half-pay each, both of whom have to work to make ends meet. They can leave the child-rearing chores up to the state in the form of public education, where children are taught how to become part of the wage system, with an entitlement mentality, passively dependent on being taken care of and told what to do by Hudge and Gudge. They are not taught to think independently or work independently. They are not taught traditional truths, but only the latest fads and fashionable ideas.

The problem is painfully clear. What's the solution? It must be to restore the family to its proper place. We need a family-based economy and a family-based social system, where both state and commerce are subordinate to the family. This solution would come to be known by the cumbersome (and for some, tiresome) title of distributism. Those who dismiss distributism out of hand at least owe the courtesy to Chesterton to find out what it is and, as importantly, what it isn't. As we further explore the rest of his writing, we will take a good look at distributism.

Two of Chesterton's most famous lines come from this book: "The Christian ideal has not been tried and found wanting. It has been found difficult and left untried,"[5] and "If a thing is worth doing, it is worth doing badly."[6] The first cannot possibly be misunderstood. The second is always misunderstood. It is not a license to be sloppy or not to strive for the best. It is praise of the amateur. While a professional may do a certain job better than the amateur, the amateur has the advantage of doing something, as the name implies, for love and not for money. The model amateur is the mother.

St. Francis of Assisi

This was the first book that Chesterton wrote after his conversion. St. Francis represented a bridge from the early part of his life to the later. Even before Chesterton came to believe in Christ, and long before he came into the Catholic Church, he felt a connection to this universal saint. Francis had always been a friend to him. When we are devoted to a saint, he is first of all, a friend. Chesterton was thankful for St. Francis for the path he helped pave to the Church, and fittingly the book is about thanksgiving. Chesterton says, "The best kind of giving is thanksgiving."[7]

St. Francis is one of the most popular saints and one of the most misunderstood. Chesterton says the world appreciates the saint but not the sanctity. His path to sanctity was utterly unexpected. He started out as a soldier and troubadour. He became a builder and beggar. Finally, he was the mirror of Christ.

Chesterton suggests (perhaps unconsciously) that only a saint can write about a saint, but the same could be said of writing about a mystic. Chesterton's exploration of St. Francis's mysticism seems to reveal an insider's perspective. After achieving a spiritual depth that would have been more than enough for the rest of us, Francis rushes further, deeper. He disappears into a cave to be alone with God. The man who came out of that cave, says Chesterton, was not the man who went in. Whatever happened to him "must remain greatly dark to most of us, [we] who are ordinary and selfish men whom God has not broken to make anew."[8] And yet interestingly enough, Chesterton *does* seem to know what it is. The mystic, he says, "passes through that moment when there is nothing but God."[9] There cannot be a more powerful—or precise—definition of mysticism than that.

> If a man saw the world upside down, with all the trees and towers hanging head downwards as in a pool, one effect would be to emphasise the idea of dependence. . . . He would be thankful to God for not dropping the whole cosmos like a vast crystal to be shattered into falling stars. Perhaps St. Peter saw the world so, when he was crucified head downwards.[10]

> In a . . . cynical sense . . . men have said, "Blessed is he that expecteth nothing, for he shall not be disappointed." It was in a wholly happy and enthusiastic sense that St. Francis said, "Blessed is he who expecteth nothing, for he shall enjoy everything." It was by this deliberate idea of starting from zero . . . that he did come to enjoy even earthly things as few people have enjoyed them.[11]

St. Francis, as a mirror of Christ, reflected the light of Christ as the moon reflects the sun. His humility prevented him from ever realizing this. He "was full of the sentiment that he had not suffered enough to be worthy even to be a distant follower of his suffering God." He did not feel he was "worthy even of the shadow of the crown of thorns."[12] But apparently he *was* worthy. St. Francis, in the most profound of mysteries, literally bore on his body the wounds of Christ. The paradox is that this poor suffering soul was one of the happiest men who ever lived.

The root of his joy was thanksgiving. St. Francis realized his utter dependence on God. Next, he set out to live for others and not for himself, to never turn his back on someone in need. He became a beggar helping other beggars, knowing that all of us are beggars. Finally, he learned to restrain himself from physical joy for the sake of spiritual joy. Indulging in material pleasures tends to make people forget God. Refraining from those pleasures has the great effect of encouraging us to remember God at every turn. St. Francis "devoured fasting as a hungry man devours food."[13] He sought poverty as other men sought wealth. He basked in humility as others bask in pride and glory. Thus, nothing that happened to him could bother him. Nothing that touched him could touch him. Nothing came between him and God.

When we realize that we owe everything to God, we live completely for God. And it is a joyful relationship we have with him. Chesterton says, "Debt and dependence do become pleasures in the presence of unspoilt love. . . . It is the key of all the problems of Franciscan morality which puzzle the merely modern mind; but above all it is the key of asceticism. It is the highest and holiest of the paradoxes that the man who really knows he cannot pay his debt will be for ever paying it. He will be for ever giving back what he cannot give back, and cannot be expected to give back. He will be always throwing things away into a bottomless pit of unfathomable thanks."[14]

St. Thomas Aquinas

In this book, Chesterton does something as ridiculous as what I'm trying to accomplish by summing up all his books in one chapter: he sums up the *Summa Theologica* in one chapter. But he does it! And in another chapter, he sums up the whole of Thomistic philosophy. It is understandable that the great Thomistic scholar—Etienne Gilson—said that this is the best book ever written on St. Thomas. The amazing thing is that Chesterton apparently never read the *Summa*. The only explanation for his insight is that he thought with the same mind as St. Thomas, drawing his wisdom from the same deep well. Or there's Evelyn Waugh's explanation: that Chesterton simply ran his fingers over the binding of the *Summa* and absorbed everything in it.

Chesterton starts out by comparing St. Francis and St. Thomas, two saints who on the surface could not be more different. In spite of their obvious contrasts, he says, "They were really doing the same thing. One of them was doing it in the world of the mind, the other was doing it in the world of the worldly.... They were doing the same great work; one in the study, the other in the street."[15] Neither of them brought anything new to Christianity. Rather, they brought Christianity closer to the kingdom of God. In the process, each of them "reaffirmed the Incarnation, by bringing God back to earth."[16]

St. Thomas was not only intent on upholding the *reality* of the Incarnation, he also wanted to show what were the *implications* of the Incarnation. Bringing Heaven and Earth together means bringing body and soul together. A man is not a man without his body, just as a man is not a man without his soul: "A corpse is not a man; but also a ghost is not a man."[17] St. Thomas thereby affirms the dogma that Modernism rejects: the resurrection of the body.

Along with rejecting the body, the Moderns also reject the mind, that is, free will, or the moral responsibility of man. Chesterton says, "Upon this sublime and perilous liberty hang heaven and hell, and all the mysterious drama of the soul."[18]

St. Thomas is the champion of God the Creator. He affirms what Scripture says, that God created the physical world and all that is in it, and said that it was *good*. As a matter of fact, says Chesterton, the work of Heaven alone was material, that is, the making of the material world, and there was nothing evil about it. The work of Hell, on the other hand, was entirely spiritual. Hell doesn't create anything. It only destroys. Thus, there are no bad things, only bad uses of things.[19]

St. Thomas introduced Aristotle into Christian philosophy. This was gigantic. But someone came along three centuries later and obscured our view of the giant St. Thomas Aquinas and, consequently, of Aristotle. It was a stout little Augustinian monk from Germany: Martin Luther. Chesterton's amazing insight is that the Reformation had less to do with faith than with philosophy. It was the revenge of the Platonists. St. Augustine, through no fault of his own, had access to Plato but not Aristotle. Martin Luther, like his fellow Augustinians, was a Platonist, tending toward a more subjective view of truth. Luther rejected that clear and ordered and objective Aristotelian philosophy to the point that he attacked reason itself. Chesterton says, "It was the very life of the Thomist teaching that Reason can be trusted: it was the very life of Lutheran teaching that Reason is utterly untrustworthy."[20] When Martin Luther attacked reason, he led the way to the epoch we now live in, the Epoch of Doubt, the Epoch of Personality, of Psychology, of Suggestion, of Advertisement. Chesterton points out that all the strange and destructive modern philosophies rose in Germany and can be traced back to Luther's break from the Catholic Church. Modern philosophy does not correspond to reality. Thomism, however, is realism in the proper understanding of the term. St. Thomas not only defends the reality of the physical world, of creation, but also the reality of life itself. And life is exactly what is doubted most in today's Culture of Death.

We are living the legacy of what Chesterton calls "the morbid Renaissance intellectual" who says, "To be or not to be—that is the question." But St. Thomas Aquinas, says Chesterton, replies in a voice of thunder, "To be—that is the answer!"[21] It evokes Chesterton's own confrontation with that question when he was a young man, when he almost gave the wrong answer.

The Everlasting Man

This is the book where Chesterton puts it all together. It is nothing less than a history of the world and all the ideas in the world, drawing on mythology, archeology, literature, legend, religion, philosophy, and any other discipline you'd like. The argument is simple. Christ is the hinge of history. The world leading up to Christ was vastly different from the world after Christ came. Christ changed everything. And the Christian explanation is the only reasonable explanation for what happened.

C. S. Lewis was an atheist until he read *The Everlasting Man*. Not only was the book largely responsible for his conversion to Christianity, it was the basis for all the arguments he uses in *Mere Christianity*.

Chesterton says that the problem with the critics of the Church is that they are too close to it to see it properly. They cannot see the big picture, only what directly affects them. With their sulking and their perversity and their petty criticism, they are merely *reacting* to the Church. What they need to do is back up. And that's what Chesterton has the reader do in this book: back up far enough and see that the Church is not narrower but broader than the universe, not predictable but unexpected.

And so we back up. We see that religion is as old as civilization. And civilization is as old as history. And history only goes as far back as history. Prehistory is veiled from us; the curtain rises on a play already in progress. Chesterton argues that it was religion that advanced civilization. It was religion that dealt with the meanings of things, with the development and interpretation of symbols, which advanced communication and knowledge, or what we call the arts and the sciences.

If we study any civilization, we see that after growth comes decay. Chesterton says men do not grow tired of evil, but of good. They become weary of joy. They stop worshipping God and start worshipping idols, their own bad imitations of God, and they become as wooden as the thing they worship. They start worshipping nature and become unnatural. They start worshipping sex and become perverted. Men start lusting after men and become unmanly. "The most ignorant of humanity know by the very look of earth that they have forgotten heaven."[22] We see it in the big picture of history but also in all the little pictures.

In the big picture, something happens in a little place that involves all the big things. "Bethlehem," says Chesterton, "is emphatically a place where extremes meet."[23]

The Gospels paint a picture of a man who was indeed a wonder-worker. He did not speak in platitudes, but in riddles and rebukes. His teachings were as difficult to accept in his own time as they are today. The critics try to create a different Christ from the one portrayed in the Gospels by picking and choosing whatever they want. They always try to make him merely human, whether they make him a socialist or a pacifist or a madman. "There must surely have been something not only mysterious but many-sided about Christ if so many smaller Christs can be carved out of him."[24]

But the main impression one gets from studying the teachings of Christ is that he really did not come to teach. What separates Christianity from other religions is that its central figure does not wish to be known merely as a teacher. He makes the greatest claim of all. Mohammed did not claim to be God. Buddha did not claim to be God. But Christ did claim to be God.

The story gets stranger still. All of Christ's life is a steady pursuit toward the ultimate sacrifice: the Crucifixion.

> All the great groups that stood about the Cross represent in one way or another the great historical truth of the time; that the world could not save itself. Man could do no more. Rome and Jerusalem and Athens and everything else . . . [25]

This central dogma of the Christian Faith, that God died, that, in Chesterton's phrase, God was for one instant forsaken of God, that God sacrificed himself to himself, is a claim more mysterious than anything, even the mystery of creation itself. But the gospel story does not end with God's death; it ends with the most startling episode of all: an empty grave and God again walking in a garden, as on the first day of creation.

It is this strange story that explains why Christianity has done something different than just survive. It has itself returned to life many times after having been apparently defeated. It has, as Chesterton says, "died many times and risen again; for it had a God who knew the way out of the grave."[26]

Chesterton's Poetry

J.C. Squire said that Chesterton's poetry "has been hidden by the dust he has raised."[27] That dust has managed to obscure an incredible output of almost one thousand poems. Of these, there are at least three that everyone should read. One of them is sixteen lines long, one is seven pages long, and the other is an entire book.

"The Donkey"

This is a sweet and simple poem about how the humble shall be exalted. We get a brief glimpse of God's glory from a donkey's point of view. Here's the whole thing:

When fishes flew and forests walked
And figs grew upon thorn,
Some moment when the moon was blood
Then surely I was born.

With monstrous head and sickening cry
And ears like errant wings,
The devil's walking parody
On all four-footed things.

The tattered outlaw of the earth,
Of ancient crooked will;
Starve, scourge, deride me: I am dumb,
I keep my secret still.

Fools! For I also had my hour;
One far fierce hour and sweet:
There was a shout about my ears,
And palms before my feet.

Lepanto

A rousing war song of pounding rhythm and vivid, interwoven images, *Lepanto* builds with steady momentum to a clash and climax like the very battle it describes. The fact that Chesterton manages to give a religion lesson and a theology lesson (the two are not the same), plus a history lesson, within the confines of a unique and creative scheme of rhyme and meter, is simply breathtaking.

Don John of Austria is one of the great, forgotten heroes of history, who led the Christian forces against the Muslim forces in a decisive sea battle in 1571 that was a turning point in European history. The Turks had controlled the Mediterranean for a century, the Crusaders had long ago been sent home defeated, and the Eastern Christian Empire had fallen to the Muslims, who were threatening to attack the Italian peninsula and take its grand prize, Rome. But the twenty-four-year-old illegitimate son of the dead Emperor Charles V gathered ships and rallied warriors from several different countries, commanding generals far older and more experienced, arming everyone, from galley slave to soldier, with a unique weapon: a rosary. He then sailed into battle and routed a superior enemy. Chesterton not only gives us a front row seat at the battle, but he provides the perspectives of the remote outsiders watching from afar, from the Turkish Sultan to the "cold queen of England" (Elizabeth I), to Mohammed himself in his Muslim paradise, to the suspicious King Philip of Spain (half brother of Don John), to Pope Pius V, and finally to one of the warriors who fought in the battle: Cervantes, who would go on to write *Don Quixote*. The poem is a complete tour de force.

> Trumpet that sayeth ha!
> *Domino gloria!*

The Ballad of the White Horse

> Before the gods that made the gods
> Had seen their sunrise pass,
> The White Horse of the White Horse Vale
> Was cut out of the grass . . .[28]

The Ballad of the White Horse is one of the last great epic poems in the English language and deserves to be studied by any student of English literature. It is the one work that Chesterton labored over more than any other.

Here he gives the spotlight to another outstanding hero that history has somehow managed to neglect. Though he is known as King Alfred the Great, the only English king with that epithet, his name is overshadowed, first by a king who is known only in legend, King Arthur, and then by a cast of royals who are either outright villains or pathetic bums. Alfred, "that oft-defeated king," valiantly saved his people from a barbarian invasion when it looked like England had completely lost. Then, after restoring Christian civilization, he nurtured the arts and education, and preserved and spread the Catholic Faith, rather than betraying it and crushing it as his successors would later do. Chesterton tells his story in clear and colorful verse, from Alfred's vision of the Blessed Virgin Mary, to the gathering of the varied and symbolic warriors who will join him in battle, to his undercover mission, posing as a balladeer in the enemy camp, to his humorous and humbling encounter with an old woman who slaps him in the face, to the fierce and thrilling battle itself, and finally to the prophetic and powerful aftermath. The poet tells us that the day will come when we will long for Alfred's time when the enemies were obvious and ideas plain. Instead we will face subtle and stealthier enemies whose weapons will be words and whose ideas will be murky.

> They shall not come with warships,
> They shall not waste with brands,
> But books be all their eating,
> And ink be on their hands . . .
>
> By terror and the cruel tales
> Of curse in bone and kin,
> By weird and weakness winning,
> Accursed from the beginning,
> By detail of the sinning,
> And denial of the sin.[29]

Civilization is hard work. It is always decaying. Unexamined theories threaten to take over the truth like weeds threaten to overgrow the image of the white horse carved into the green turf of the English hillside.

Chesterton's Journalism

Above all else, Chesterton considered himself a journalist, the most ephemeral of all who call themselves writers. The bulk of his literary efforts were published on the back of advertisements designed to be thrown away. But his words survive.

The four papers where he was a regular columnist represent four distinct styles of journalism, though all the writing is distinctively GKC: the *Daily News*, which more than anything else established his early reputation; the *Illustrated London News*, which gave him a noteworthy position that he held for over three decades; the *New Witness*, which was his brother's highly-charged political paper that Gilbert took over as editor; and finally *G. K.'s Weekly*, which was his own unique paper. His contributions to these papers account for almost 4,000 of his 5,000-plus essays. The task of producing these essays on a regular basis, in addition to all the other writing and speaking he did, is hardly possible to comprehend. Nor is the fact—which was attested to by all of his secretaries—that he could write two essays at the same time: dictating one while writing a completely different one in longhand. There is another account of how when he was being moved from his flat in Battersea, he was writing an essay and had to keep switching to a different piece of furniture as each was being hauled out of the room, till finally he was using the mantelpiece. The whole while he was being interviewed by a reporter, C. A. Dawson-Scott. When he finished, he folded the essay, put it in an envelope, handed it to the other journalist and asked him to deliver it to the editor of the *Daily News*.

Daily News (1901–1913)

The *Daily News* essays offer some of the most delightful of Chesterton's writing, as he burst onto the literary scene with confidence and creativity. He began as a book reviewer taking on texts by both the famous and the forgettable. He wrote on Kipling, Khayyam, Stevenson, Yeats, Shakespeare, Schopenhauer, George MacDonald, Rostand, Ruskin, Carlyle, Tennyson, Walter Scott, Browning, Byron, the Brontës, Cervantes, Tolstoy, Shelley, Dickens, Walt Whitman, and someone named Shaw. He came to the rescue of form against fashion, of delight against despair, of robust verse against "the poetry of emotional collapse," and bold faith against snide doubt. He chose to cross swords with the modern world and its "appalling absence of joy."[30] His politics spilled over into his art as politics always do. He defended democracy and the common man against the snobs and aristocrats in the studio and in the street. "Democracy," he says, "cannot be conducted as a tame, mechanical, utilitarian thing, the final solution of social problems. If it is to be conducted at all, it must be conducted as a religion was, as a heroic enterprise, as an immortal battle, and an everlasting crisis."[31]

He defended the natural ideal of patriotism against the stilted and artificial ideals of humanitarianism.

> It seems to me one of the oldest and idlest mistakes to suppose that we come nearer to men by ignoring those very partialities which make life tolerable to them. To love humanity while despising patriotism is to love the bodies of the peoples and to despise their souls. If we are broad enough to share all the dominant traits of humanity we must primarily share its narrowness. A man is far more closely linked with the life of nature by loving his own children than by attempting to yearn over the youthful boa constrictor or dandle the infant rhinoceros.[32]

He said that we would not complain of materialism "if common-sense were only common."[33] It is an observation he would make of many more modern philosophies over the next three-plus decades. But here sound the clear notes of his chorus for the first time.

In his third year on the paper, he was still engaging his readers with surprising twists on familiar subjects and defying most of the trends that were being accelerated and celebrated everywhere else. He defended patriotism but criticized imperialism (which meant opposing the Boer War), defended the preservation of rural life against the creeping urban life, and defended liberalism while criticizing liberals. He saw a coming loss of freedom and a coming loss of character. Not yet thirty years old, he was already a master essayist, writing "short articles on huge subjects." He wrote "with one great hope, that of arousing controversy."[34]

And nothing is more controversial than religion. "Religious liberty means (apparently) that no one is allowed to speak of important matters at all. All that our modern tolerance has done is to put the saint in the same dungeon with the heresiarch. Then we talk about the weather, and call it the absolute liberation of all the creeds."[35]

What are the essentials of a great religion? Chesterton told us forthrightly. It is "decisive" and "paradoxical." It covers "the whole of life" and speaks "as if from outside it." Above all, it has "the two supreme and indispensable marks of a great religion; firstly, it [is] regarded by most people as funny, and secondly it really [is] funny." A great religion "must have forms, festivals, music, and arrogance, like the Roman Church or the Salvation Army . . . must, if it [is] to have faith, learn to play the fool." It is absurd to say that a man is "ready to toil or die for his convictions when he [is] not even ready to wear a wreath round his head for it."[36]

No one expected him to write about religion in a secular newspaper, but he wrote about religion in a way no one expected.

Not surprising, then, that he said religion must be paradoxical. Chesterton was already becoming famous for his paradoxes, and many of his readers and admirers assumed that he was being merely paradoxical by defending religion in general and Christianity in particular. But the jovial Chesterton was quite serious even if he was quite funny. "All paradoxers, if they be also honest men, are aiming joyfully at their own destruction. We have paradoxes, and it is our effort, day and night, to turn them into truisms."[37] What he is striving to achieve is not the paradox, but the platitude. "Every man who is fighting for his own beliefs is fighting to take it away from himself. He may be clever in dull places and important in mean places; but in the land that he desires he will be nothing—a reed with the reeds in the river."[38] A truism is a popular truth, a paradox an unpopular one. But they are both true.

All of these essays are controversial. That is, Chesterton stood in favor of a truth he identified against an error he also identified. "In persuasion we have nothing to do except to try and show that we are right." To what end? "What we are all trying to do is to induce some regiments of the enemy to desert."[39]

And fifteen years before his conversion he wrote, "The Catholic Church is attacked because it is Catholic, and defended because it is Catholic."[40]

When he began being referred to as the Prince of Paradox, he, of course, protested that title. Though he was accused of turning everything around, he was only making observations of how turned around everything in our world is. We treat work as play and treat play as work. Politics are not taken seriously but sports are. Work is supposed to be a labor, but instead play has become a labor, filled with regimental training and the bursting of veins. We insist on analyzing everything, taking it apart, when everything is already falling apart and needs to be put back together.

We rely on machines, and so put our trust in science. But the one lesson that science really *can* teach us is one we have not learned. "The one important truth in mechanics is this: that the most idealistic work is the most practical work."[41] The man who makes wheels for your car, after all, has to make them as ideally and perfectly round as he can. "He would be a fool if he sat down in the middle of the road and cried because they never could be perfectly round in the sight of God. But he would be much more of a fool if he did not aim at exquisite mathematical roundness. He would be much more of a fool if he put the car on top of four shapeless shapes called in Euclid irregular polygons, and in popular language smashed window frames, and if he expected to win a race with a machine so constructed."[42] If he said that he was not an idealist or theorist, that he was not going to waste his time doing abstract calculations, but nonetheless, he was going to win the race, we would not share his confidence. So we are wrong when we say that ideals are not practical.

What else do we get wrong? Health care. That is, we have turned health care into prevention rather than cure. Because it is not possible to foresee all possible evils a long time before they happen or modify or avert them without exertion and without harming anything or anybody, it turns out that prevention is not better than the cure. Prevention is an enemy of liberty besides being a gigantic nuisance. "Cure is healthy; because it is effected at an unhealthy moment. Prevention is unhealthy; because it is done at a healthy moment."[43]

There is another thing we get wrong. Death. That is, we try to ignore it, even to the point of avoiding the pain that others go through who have to deal with the death of their loved ones. We simply try to smooth it over. But Chesterton says, "The one way to make bereavement tolerable is to make it important. To gather your friends, to have a gloomy festival, to talk, to cry, to praise the dead—all that does change the atmosphere, and carry human nature over the open grave. The nameless torture is to try and treat it as something private and casual, as our elegant stoics do. That is at once pride and pain and hypocrisy. The only way to make less of death is to make more of it."[44]

A better title for Chesterton may be the General of Generalization. The paradoxes arise often because so many of our generalizations are wrong, whereas Chesterton's generalizations are right. He warned against the bad generalization. For instance, we should not say "most people are stupid." That's stupid. It is like saying "most people are tall." Obviously, "tall" can only mean taller than most people. "It is absurd," says Chesterton, "to denounce the majority of mankind as below the average of mankind."[45]

Because we do not know how to generalize, we do not know how to argue. Chesterton, the Count of Controversialists, shows us how. We not only have to get the truth right, we have to get the proportions right. Most arguments, he points out, "are not about what is true, but about what is important, if true. Sanity does not consist in seeing things; madmen see things more clearly than other people. Sanity consists in seeing the big things big and the small things small."[46]

After a decade's worth of his essays for the _Daily News_, where G. K. Chesterton reviewed both classic and contemporary literature, writing on art and angels, on poetry and pessimists, on Christianity and common sense, he started shifting his emphasis from grand, general ideas to more pointed and particular ones, as he identified some monstrous modern evils. Or perhaps we should say it is one evil with many adjectives. It is something that no one else seemed to see. It is more obvious now than it was a hundred years ago, but we still manage to ignore it. It is tyranny: academic and political and economic tyranny. "Nobody sees the largest danger of our age: it is too simple. It is simply that the rich are slowly enslaving the poor, partly by industrial despotism, partly by scientific benevolence, partly by State officialism."[47]

We often give up our freedom because freedom means doing things for ourselves, which is a great bother. We stop working for ourselves and work for someone else who will take care of us. We stop ruling ourselves because it is easier and even safer to have someone else rule us. We stop thinking for ourselves because we find it simpler to have someone else think for us. Then we wake up one morning and find that we are slaves to institutions that are far out of our control.

In the academic world, the timeless truths are no longer taught. Instead, we are subject to the insanity of faddish philosophies, deconstruction, relativism, and political correctness. "Our professors (as their name implies) merely profess profligate nonsense."[48] They cannot ask plain questions, because in their skepticism and agnosticism, they cannot accept plain answers. It comes from a loss of common sense and a loss of tradition, which often amount to the same thing.

We keep a tradition, says Chesterton, not because it is old, but because it is nice. It is only because it has been kept, generation after generation, that it manages to get old. We can treat it as an old thing, but not as a dead thing. It is a living thing as long as we keep it. But, more and more, we are killing our traditions.

> Common-sense, the oldest thing in history, has put all children under the authority of their parents. It does this for two unanswerable reasons. First, that to let a child alone is to murder it. Second, that Nature has inspired two unpaid persons with a fantastic taste for taking care of it. But common-sense also says that there are exceptions; and that when the two persons

are blood-drinkers or devil-worshippers, or have a taste in torture, the children should be taken away and the child-torturers very severely punished. I do not wonder they were severely punished; I can imagine them savagely punished. I not only understand that cruel parents may be imprisoned; I can, with a stretch of historic imagination, conceive their being burned at the stake. Such hatred of one's own flesh has in it something mysterious and unfathomably shameful; and starts alive that same nerve of loathing that leaped back from witchcraft or that cries aloud at sexual perversion. Nothing, one would think, could be simpler or saner than that the tribe should make an example of such demoniac abusers of the family. Democracy is right when it stands for the normal; not when it stands for the average.[49]

In 1912, the paper that gave G. K. Chesterton his voice started losing its own voice. When newspapers support a particular political party, and when the leadership of that party is exposed as being corrupt, the paper has a decision to make: either stand up boldly for what is right in spite of the party, or stand up stupidly for the party in spite of what is right. The Liberal Party controlled Parliament but some of its most powerful players got caught in the case of insider trading known as the Marconi Scandal. Instead of cleaning house, ousting those politicians, and making an example of them, the Party used its majority to excuse the key players at the conclusion of a hearing on the matter. The guilty players made a humbling but mumbling public apology without admitting any wrongdoing, and got away with a slap on the wrist. Everyone knew it was a whitewash, and most of the papers said as much, some more loudly than others, but the *Daily News* failed to condemn the scandal for what it was.

It is commonly thought that Chesterton was fired from the *Daily News* for raising his voice against the Liberal Party, but the fact is, he quit—after calling the publisher (in a poem) a cad and a coward. His leaving the *Daily News* was itself news. But even before he quit, we can see a change in tone during the last months of his tenure there, especially when he devoted one of his columns to an open letter to the Liberal Party. In it, he confessed that for the first time since he started writing for the paper, he was not enjoying himself. He admitted that he had been a Liberal "since shortly before [he] was born" because the party represented freedom and democracy. He saw, however, that it was clearly acting in the direct opposite of those ideals.

As in his early days at the *Daily News*, he still brought up literature, but even here there was a noticeable change. He offered a criticism of some modern writers, Kipling, the barely-remembered Israel Zangwill, and the now largely-forgotten Hall Caine, as being brilliant writers who lost something when they stopped writing about the universe and started writing about the world. In some ways, and certainly for some people, this was about the same time that Chesterton himself succumbed to the same thing. His writing became less universal and more particular. He went from the universe and its glories to the world and its problems. But unlike his "realistic" colleagues, Chesterton did not simply describe the problems; he offered some solutions.

> We say that . . . an owner would be in a simpler and honester attitude to the whole universe. He would say, "I know the fruit of my acts and the limits of my responsibility. I know whom I am serving: I am serving myself, my wife and children, and what I can give beyond the necessary I will give to such a God as I may truly worship or such a public policy as I may truly approve." But as things are in a complex wage-earning

society (whether capitalist or collectivist in its form), no
man of any trade really knows for whose benefit he has
done one single stroke of his work. . . . Our work is not
simple enough to have any sense in it. The meaning has
gone out of our daily actions; and our very gestures are
void and vain.[50]

He also heroically defended Home Rule for Ireland, which
again was something his ruling party opposed. Chesterton called
out the unnatural position of the Englishman that has led to a
permanent persecution of the Irish people. His analysis was acute
and prophetic. The ideas which are "now believed tolerantly,
casually," that were "once held savagely but now only sanely"[51]
are first the theory of the triumphant Teuton, second the horror
of the Roman religion, and third the belief in commerce and the
contempt for agriculture. These beliefs would not only lead to
the horrors of Nazi Germany, but the horrors the world is now
experiencing.

We have put our trust in man, not in God. And we have put
our trust in gold. "And what shall we answer? I confess I can only
answer in that lamentable sort of language used when religious
differences were very marked: that if our God be God He can
deliver us out of this furnace, but if not, we will not worship a
golden image that such men have set up; that the safety of the
proud insults heaven; and that idols are not always empty, but
are the houses of devils."[52]

The end came in February of 1913 when Chesterton broke
with the paper and the party, both of which he had served
loyally. He learned the hard lesson that the people in power
cannot be trusted and that we cannot expect political solutions
to the problems that plague us.

Illustrated London News (1905–1936)

> I do not doubt for a moment that the young idealists who ask for Indian independence are very fine fellows; most young idealists are fine fellows. I do not doubt for an instant that many of our Imperial officials are stupid and oppressive; most Imperial officials are stupid and oppressive. But when I am confronted with the actual papers and statements of the Indian Nationalists I feel much more dubious, and, to tell the truth, a little bored. The principal weakness of Indian Nationalism seems to be that it is not very Indian and not very national.

It was September 18, 1909, when those words appeared in Chesterton's weekly column in the *Illustrated London News*. He would go on to argue that it made more sense for those who called themselves Indian Nationalists to insist on their own ancient culture rather than on the culture invented for them by someone else. When a young Indian lawyer read those words he immediately translated the whole essay and published it widely throughout his native region. He thus began a movement that would eventually lead to Indian independence. His name was Mohandas Gandhi.

The *Illustrated London News* is where Chesterton found his largest and most steady audience. He spun out a weekly column for over thirty-one years, writing for the general public (and a regular paycheck). His essays were generally "safe" but offered an enormous variety, the exception being the war propaganda during World War I.

Ironically, when he was hired by the paper, he was told he could write about anything he wanted "except politics and religion." And that's pretty much all he ever wrote about. We see Chesterton in all his glorious political incorrectness, opposing votes for women, defending drinking and smoking,

mocking popular social reform, questioning the honesty of the
rich, and defending giving money to beggars. "Nothing will be
done until we have realized that charity is not giving rewards
to the deserving, but happiness to the unhappy."[53] As for the
female suffragists, Chesterton said he could accept the idea of
women voting; he just could not accept any of the reasons that
the suffragists gave for women voting. He saw no reason to bring
women into a system that was completely corrupt. Chesterton,
the ardent defender of democracy, was the endless critic of the
current political process. The politician, he said, is always the
enemy of the crowds. "His whole career has only two stages:
first, as quickly as possible to represent his town; then as quickly
as possible to misrepresent it."[54]

Just as political questions cannot be avoided, neither can
religious questions: "No intellectual movements, however
searching, no logical processes, however severe, can ever alter
this ultimate possibility; for all such intellectual movements and
logical processes bring us at last to the edge of what is called the
Unknowable; and there our poetic curiosity begins."[55] Moreover,
Chesterton said, "Every political question is a religious question."
Chesterton even starts hinting at a sacramental understanding of
things: "Whenever men really believe that they can get to the
spiritual, they always employ the material. When the purpose is
good, it is bread and wine; when the purpose is evil, it is eye of
newt and toe of frog."[56]

In the opening decade of the twentieth century, most people
were looking ahead with great optimism. Communication
and transportation were experiencing great breakthroughs.
New scientific disciplines were being developed. The great
educational institutions were flourishing. New technology
would provide clear sailing. But Chesterton saw rough waves
ahead. He said, "We men and women are all in the same boat,
upon a stormy sea. We owe to each other a terrible and tragic

loyalty."[57] As early as 1909, he saw war coming with Germany. He was distressed that in Europe, where all countries share a fundamental heritage and should share the same basic philosophy, there was already a war of ideas that posed a threat to Christian civilization.

He distrusted the newfangled academic disciplines: "It is certainly a just and humane act to rescue any human beings from having sociology taught to them."[58] He worried that "ethics" were replacing "morals" in an attempt to treat human conduct scientifically and not theologically. And "ethics" were already turning into "ethology," which Chesterton regarded as part of "a curiously bloodless and polysyllabic style now adopted for the discussion of the most direct and intimate matters."[59]

Darwinism and Marxism epitomized the new authority of science and economics, but Chesterton was not impressed. Scientific and economic theories do not explain mankind. They only reveal the prejudices of the people who employ them. "When learned men begin to use their reason," said Chesterton, "then I generally discover that they haven't got any."[60]

He noticed subtle and not-so-subtle attacks on the family, and his defense of the family is all the more prophetic today: "Most human experience goes to show that the more a family is really a family the better it is—that is, the more it really consists of father, mother, and children." He found himself having to defend common things and the common man, including the idea of property as "that which is proper to man."[61]

He also explained the vacuity of today's debates. People cannot argue using either reason or authority: they have "neither the courage to assert a thing nor the capacity to prove it, so [they] allude to it in a light and airy style, as if somebody else had asserted and proved it already." Or, in other words, "referring to the very thing that is in dispute as if it were now beyond dispute."[62]

Chesterton explained how to conduct an argument:

> This world is full of truths, half-truths, probabilities, and possibilities of various orders of validity and pointing in various directions. But there are some facts which are certain in a quite special way; and if other facts contradict them, then we must inquire into the other facts; but we must not waste our time inquiring into the one fact which is certain...all good argument begins with the indisputable thing and then disputing everything else in light of it.[63]

His loyalty to his fellow travelers on the boat was demonstrated by his willingness to argue with them. He saw their bad ideas as imperiling everyone else on board. He was constant and consistent in his defense of Christianity, morality, and liberty because they are inextricably tied together. Defending morality means defending liberty. It is the one preaching immorality who will destroy the rights of the free man and sink the boat that all of us are in together.

One constant theme of these weekly essays is the difficulty of defending the normal. We could almost say it is the disappearance of the normal, which Chesterton noticed everywhere. He got on a train and noticed that there was a first-class carriage and a third-class carriage. That would seem to imply that there is a second-class carriage. But there isn't. "It is typical of our time," he said, "that the middle thing has been knocked out. The central, the normal is sacrificed. The middle class is going or gone."[64]

It is difficult to speak idealistically about the middle class. But it is impossible and ridiculous to have to choose between extremes, between Tweedledee and Tweedledum, between Scylla and Charybdis. "We are not merely asked to choose between things equally bad, [but] between things that are exactly the same."[65] Defending the normal is difficult when even normal speech has been jarred. People abuse language along with reason. "They contradict the dictionary more than they do the Bible."[66]

From one side, Chesterton saw that Prohibition was coming—a Puritan attack on one of the normal pleasures of man. But from the other side, he saw the pagans attacking the normal. And the barbarians, too.

In 1912, the great *Titanic* sank. Chesterton saw the tragedy as a symbol of the age—the "sinking of an unsinkable ship," the pride before the fall, the "touch of over-civilization which is always the first touch of a returning barbarism."[67]

This barbarism can be seen in the loss of respect for human rights but also in the weird new respect for animal rights. The new nature worship has no limits, and the sympathy with earth and animals has no verifiable results; whereas if they direct their efforts "against real and certain wrongs," they "might release millions of men from the rack of . . . agony."[68]

Chesterton was most prophetic in defending that normal thing called marriage against bizarre attacks, such as the attempt to redefine it: "If we do not yet know what marriage is, doubtless it would be well to find out; though many generations of men seem to have been occupied in the inquiry in its most practical and scientific form."[69] He had no hesitation in ridiculing the "immoralists" who attacked marriage, because they represented no imaginable ideal: "I do not myself think it is wrong to laugh even at a morality in which I do believe. I most certainly think it right to laugh at a morality in which I don't believe. And I shall certainly laugh my longest and loudest about a morality that nobody has yet discovered."[70]

But he saw that there was no forum in which the normal man's voice might be heard. "The only judge of ordinary intelligence is—ordinary intelligence,"[71] but this judge has been banished from the court of opinion. The heretics are not persecuted because they are the ones in power. It is the normal man who is persecuted, who is imprisoned because he cannot afford to pay a fine, who is punished for making speeches because he has not the money to publish books.

Chesterton was loyal to the common man, loyal to the normal, but "in the last intellectual resort" he knew that loyalty "is only due to that yet higher thing that made all of us and is above us all."[72] And that is where the real battle rages. "If you are loyal to anything and wish to preserve it, you must recognise that it has or might have enemies; and you must hope that the enemies will fail."[73]

In his 1910 book on William Blake, G. K. Chesterton says that we all wake up on a battlefield, a reference to the spiritual warfare into which each of us is born. Five years later, Chesterton had a rather more direct sensation of that experience. He had had a complete physical collapse at the end of 1914, and almost six months later emerged from a semi-comatose state to full consciousness to find his country in the midst of World War I. He woke up fighting, but the landscape of the whole world had changed.

In his first essay upon his return, he announced that he did not want to write about the war; he wanted to write about everything else.[74] But for the next three and a half years, with increasing and narrowing specificity, most of his columns would be about the war.

Chesterton defined what the war was about. Germany was the modern world. It was the culmination of four centuries of deteriorating philosophy, growing materialism, fragmented thinking, and a steady decline from Catholic Europe. It was the product of the "German professors" but also of leaders who had embraced a theory of racial superiority. Chesterton said it was a war with the old dragon who must be defeated. "If our cause is wrong, it is wrong because of the vanities, self-deceptions, and jealousies of civilised human beings."[75] But it will not be wrong because of the wrong theory of man and of the souls of men. Which is why he warned, "We must greatly purify ourselves even to be worthy of this war."[76]

Recent historians, whose business it is to rewrite history, have argued that America should not have entered World War I. And some have even argued that England should not have entered that war. Strange to say, I have not found any historians who argue that Germany should not have entered the war. It seems that the case can only be made for Germany's enemies to have stayed out of the war, in which case—it certainly would have been a quick victory instead of a long defeat.

The historians base their arguments on a cold, detached analysis of political gains versus losses. But it would be a good education for them (and for everyone else) to read G. K. Chesterton's *Illustrated London News* essays written during this time. They would gain a perspective beyond the political, territorial, and material interests of the war. They would understand firsthand the philosophies that were being attacked and defended. "At the back of all modern history," wrote Chesterton, "is that war with the barbarians which filled the Dark Ages and has returned in our own."[77] He saw Christendom was under attack by an enemy who had embraced a non-Christian, Norse heritage, who was swept away by racial theories of superiority, and who operated without the restraints of common Christian decency. They no longer believed that warfare should be confined to the battlefield and to soldiers, but that it could include "the butchery of unarmed and unoffending folk"[78] (e.g., Germany's torpedoing of the passenger ship *Lusitania* and its atrocities on civilians during its unprovoked invasion of Belgium).

Chesterton certainly wanted peace, but he had no time for pacifists. "Man is not a fighting animal; he is fighting because he is not an animal; he is fighting long after any animal would have fled."[79] He saw the pacifists as doing nothing but giving aid and comfort to the enemy. He appealed to a universal standard of right and wrong with real villains and real heroes. There is a difference between St. George and the Dragon. And anyone who cannot see that is "much too impartial to be just."[80] He wanted Germany to be punished for its crimes, but more importantly he wanted it to repent for its sins. He wanted victory in the war, but more important than conquest was conversion: "Conquest may produce bitterness, but conversion produces no bitterness. It can produce nothing but gratitude, if it is conversion at all."[81]

Chesterton kept writing about the war even after the war was over. There are two reasons for this. First, Chesterton did not think the war *was* over. The end of the fighting is not peace. Peace settlements are not peace. The Prussian philosophy had not been defeated. He warned that "at the first chance Prussia, at the head of all her slaves, would return to the charge."[82] That is precisely what happened. Chesterton explained the future better than historians explain the past.

Secondly, there is one episode in the war that he did not mention in these columns, but it explains in part his "intolerance for the tale ending wrong."[83] His brother Cecil died in a French military hospital just after the war ended.

There is another history-as-it-happened lesson in these pages, one that is equally prophetic. Consider this apparently universal observation from Chesterton:

> It is obvious that a politician often passes the first half of his life in explaining that he can do something, and the second half of it in explaining that he cannot. When he is in opposition he is an expert on the means to some end; and when he is in office he is an expert on the obstacles to it. In short, when he is impotent he proves to us that the thing is easy; and when he is omnipotent he proves that it is impossible.[84]

Who is the politician he is referring to? None other than Lenin. Chesterton was watching the early unfolding of the Soviet Union in the wake of the Bolshevik Revolution, and one of the first things he noticed was how quickly the Communists were compromising on their Communist ideals. What he predicted would happen was the growth of a rigid bureaucracy. Guess what happened.

Chesterton turned his attention from the Prussians to the Russians. The upheaval of civilization in the twentieth century was well underway, as we would move from international crisis to international crisis. If crises were more local, they would be more manageable. But no one seemed to have thought of that. Well, one person did.

In most histories of the twentieth century, the Second World War is regarded as the event that broke the century in two, broke the world in two, broke civilization in two. But the break occurred earlier. As G. K. Chesterton predicted, World War II, which he did not live to see, was only the unfinished business of World War I, which he correctly said was not concluded.

Chesterton's description of that fractured world in the wake of the war is a vivid description of today's still broken world. Christendom had been attacked from within and without. The assault came not only on the Faith, but on the family, on the philosophy of civilization, on everything solid and normal in our culture. The weeds that have grown through the cracks in our civilization have turned into a jungle. The growth of both big government and big business (remember Hudge and Gudge?) entangles every aspect of our lives, strangling the proper growth of religion, domesticity, and common sense. Reading Chesterton's *Illustrated London News* columns from the 1920s is much more enlightening than reading any of today's newspapers and a much more accurate description and explanation of what is going on now than anything being written now.

> Nowadays neither voters nor representatives are
> watched at all, because the whole thing has become
> too complicated and secretive to follow; and because
> everything depends on interviews and intrigues, and
> unrecorded conversations and unofficial compromises.
> Things are not watched, because there are a thousand
> evasions by advertisement and suggestion, by false
> news and fictitious biography; and, under cover of
> these things, men whom we cannot restrain pursue
> aims that we do not know.[85]

He described "a scheme of official control which is too
ambitious for human life" that had broken down and given us
"a bureaucracy that is something very near to anarchy."[86]

He also described both the glory and gore of science, which
on the one hand had given us "the beautiful vision of aviation,"
where, like the Psalmist, we could take the wings of the morning
to abide in the uttermost parts of the sea, but on the other hand
had given us the abomination of eugenics, where children (and
anyone else for that matter) could be slaughtered for the sake
of convenience. "Any advance in science," said Chesterton,
"leaves morality in its ancient balance; and it depends still on
the inscrutable soul of man whether any discovery is mainly
a benefit or mainly a calamity."[87] The Culture of Death was
already upon us a century ago. The new technologies suddenly
presented efficient, pervasive, and unimaginable ways to kill
others (and ourselves), but we faced "exactly the same spiritual
problem . . . as that which confronted Cain, when he stood with
a ragged stone in his hand." Already there was talk of abortion,
which Chesterton described as a "more than usually barbaric
form of birth control," which goes against every instinct and
"the common conscience of men."[88] He said it should be called
by its real name: "murder at its worst; not only the brand of

Cain but the brand of Herod. We expect the protest to be full
of the honour of men, of the memory of mothers, of the natural
love of children."[89] Yes, we expect it still.

Art and literature have become depraved, and yet the artists
howl in protest when they are rebuked by Christian critics,
even though their art is an open insult to God and man. The
problem with the artists, says Chesterton, is that they have no
first principles: "They have not the mastery of sorrow and sin,
because they have not made up their minds what is sin, or even
what is sorrow. They have only the passive mood that we call
passion."[90] The modern writer "does not know what he thinks;
and has a faint hope of finding out by describing how he feels.
Hence we have mere description of sensations, including sensual
sensations, for their own sake."[91]

Progress has become an ideal, even though its goal is not
defined, which makes the word meaningless. The modern world
uses the word without comprehension. "Its notion of progress
has been to pile one thing on top of another, without caring if
each thing was crushed in turn. People forgot that the human
soul can enjoy a thing most when there is time to think about
it and be thankful for it. And by crowding things together they
lost the sense of surprise; and surprise is the secret of joy."[92]

As we move further into the 1920s, the common theme of
GKC's columns was the effect of increasing secularization in
what was once a Christian society.

As usual, Chesterton was prophetic about small things—
describing the telephone as a great scientific invention, but
also "a horrible nuisance"[93]—and about big things: "There is a
very real problem of religious liberty ahead of us, though most
people seem to be strangely blind to it."[94] The looming problem
of religious liberty, he said, arises from the fact that "differences
are indeed fewer, but are much more fundamental," even more
"absolute and abysmal." We do not notice them because "a

habit of morals remains after a change of faith; sometimes only because a shell of manners remains after a loss of morals."[95]

Thus, we have the new value of "tolerance" to paste a veneer of good behavior over the absence of a definable philosophy, a belief that doesn't know what it believes, but only knows what it doesn't believe. But, said Chesterton, "secular impartiality is not so easy as it looks."[96] It purports to be neutral about religion, but it ends up persecuting religion. Those who happen to disagree with the secularists will be regarded as almost lunatic, while those who agree will seem perfectly simple and quite sensible. But there will be no basis for either the agreement or the disagreement. "Those who merely denounce intolerance seem to have no theory at all with which to defend toleration."[97]

This secularization will creep into the Faith itself. We will hear the term "True Christianity," which means the jettisoning of any distinctive Christian doctrine and the inclusion of "every sort of heathenry."

> Men reform a thing by removing the reality from it, and then do not know what to do with the unreality that is left. Thus they would reform religious institutions by removing the religion. They do not seem to see that to take away the creed and leave the servants of the creed is simply to go on paying servants for nothing. To keep the temple without the god is to be hag-ridden with superstitious vigilance about a hollow temple—about a mere shell made of brick or stone. To support the palace and not support the king is simply to pay for an empty palace.[98]

It began, ironically, with Puritanism, which took a negative form of Christianity and led to Prohibition. The reaction against the Prohibition was an outbreak of hedonism. Yet, Prohibition never went away. Chesterton predicted it would come to smokers next, and any minor pleasure would be attacked, against the will of the people. "If our government were really a representative government it would not be a meddlesome government."[99] In the meantime, the real problem—sin—will be ignored.

The world suffers, he said, "from a certain tail-foremost trick of thought.... It takes the trivial thing first and tries to put it right, without caring whether it is putting the important thing wrong." The tail wags the dog. Thus, we obsess over the intermediate and neglect the eternal. Efficiency and progress are secondary things. So are money and sex. The notion of progress, of always going forward, is especially worrisome when we have come to the end of the precipice. Chesterton suggested that at that point, retreat is a better strategy.

How did we reach this state of affairs? Through an "ignorance of the past combined with fatalism about the future."[100] What we could actually learn from the past would be very useful for creating our future:

> There might be worse fates for us than the Decline and Fall of the Roman Empire. It would have been much worse for the old heathen empire if it had not declined and fallen, but only risen higher and grown richer in its old heathen way. What would have been the good of tracing amphitheatres larger than the amphitheatre of the Coliseum? What would have been the use of building baths more elaborate than the Baths of Caracalla? What, relatively speaking, would have been the advantage even of making taller aqueducts for grander fountains or longer roads for larger legions? This is exactly what corresponds to the modern vista of scientific improvement; of quickening our quickest modes of transport, or linking up yet

closer our network of communications; of something
more rapid than racing-cars or more ubiquitous than
wireless telegraphy. We can see at this distance that
increasing the old heathen machinery would not have
made the heathen world happy; and we know in our
hearts that increasing the modern machinery will not
make the modern world happy.[101]

As the 1920s came to an end, Chesterton pointed out the
implications of our transition from a rural to an urban culture,
which happened not only because the countrymen went to the
towns, but, what was worse, the town school teacher went to
the country. He saw the ugly sameness coming, epitomized by
modern urban architecture, where the fashion-makers decree to
their followers that "their practical dwelling-place must not be
beautiful."[102] He warned about our infatuation with amazing
new technology ("The modern multiplication of wonder does
not always lead to the increase of wonder."[103]) Consider teenage
zombies texting each other during movies, dinner, and while
adults are trying to have conversations with them. Chesterton
had already considered it: "No talking that can be called talking
is conducted in a language in which there is no literature."[104]

He saw not only the loss of character, but the loss of characters,
of unique and interesting and colorful individuals who had depth
and dignity to them. If we want to see character and characters
again, "we are much more likely to find it in Christians who
accepted the Imitation of Christ than in all these millions of
materialists who are taught to imitate each other."[105]

In the academic realm, Chesterton saw the rise to prominence
of the study of economics, but noticed that "the economist
does not teach economics; he teaches the economic theory of
history."[106] Economists now claim to be scientists, and both
claim to deal with fundamentals, but Chesterton reminded
them that if they wish to get down to fundamentals, they must

begin with the fundamental problem of evil. They must deal with sin, and "sin, whatever else it is, is not merely the dregs of a bestial existence.... The worst things in man are only possible in man."[107]

Science cannot account for sin. It cannot explain the mysteries of the Faith. But Chesterton did not see a conflict between science and religion:

> Science cannot contradict religion, in the sense that scientific truth cannot contradict religious truth. That is only another way of saying that truth cannot contradict truth. But sham science and false religion can contradict each other, or corroborate each other, or do anything they choose. But in so far as the fashionable phrase was always used to mean that material science, in modern times, has been directed only against dogmas, and not against moral ideals, it is utterly and hopelessly false. The really interesting thing to notice is that the materialistic philosophy drawn from science, so far as it went, was much more destructive of the most modern ideals than of the mediaeval ideals. I do not admit that any such moral can be drawn from any material facts. But in so far as there was a moral, it was entirely immoral. And in so far as it was immoral, it was specially against the most recent humanitarian morality. It was not in the same sense, and indeed it could not be, against the abstract affirmations of a supernatural system.[108]

Most of the academic and political and economic and scientific realms deny the supernatural system. And so they continue to offer explanations of the world that fail to explain. "When people see what they do not understand they do not even believe what they see. They see what they expect; they see what they do understand, even if it is not there to be seen."[109]

Ironically, technology is easy to understand. It is certainly easy to understand when it does not work. When an airplane fails, it fails very obviously. "But the bad social system may fail because it endures. Slavery, for instance, endured for centuries of high civilisation; and yet some of us are bold enough to say it was a bad system."[110] The same could be said (and will be said) for a social system that kills babies and deviates from the definition of family. In such a failed system, we cannot condemn a thing as immoral because someone else is touting it as being "in advance of the age" and telling us that morals change.

What does finally bring a social system to an end? "A social system is always destroyed by the thing that it does not understand—the thing that it has too long left out of account."[111]

Neglecting to deal with our sins will eventually destroy us. And in a world that generally denies sin, we generally neglect to deal with it. On those exceptional occasions when we do deal with it, we deal with exceptional sin. We don't just deal with it, we dwell on it. We do not make the "obvious distinction between the general sins of men and the perverted sins of madmen."[112] But when horror strikes, we run to the Church for comfort. We know in our hearts that the only thing worse than the crimes, let alone confessions of crimes, is "the spiritual insolence that refuses to confess anything."[113]

> In order to suppress false doctrine, we must have a definition of true doctrine. And very few people now know exactly what doctrine is true, even if they feel a great many current ones are false...it is, after all, a moral doctrine which declares that mere appeals to mere appetites are wrong. It is a moral doctrine most decent people vaguely feel, but now a little too vaguely to be applied vigilantly. . . . They do emphatically involve immortal and unalterable truth. The fact that a chaotic and ill-educated time cannot clearly grasp

that truth does not alter the fact that it always will be the truth.[114]

Our "chaotic and ill-educated time," he said, is not concerned with dogmas, but with diet, "or rather with the idea of forcibly interfering with the diet of other people."[115] It suffers from "the journalistic curse" of being obsessed with the latest news, which means only hearing the end of the story without having heard the beginning of it. It rejects tradition because it is old. It assumes religion is not "up-to-date." It cuts itself off from the past, claiming to teach by experiment but refusing to learn by experience.

Chesterton insisted that all truth is connected to one truth, that all beautiful images are shadows of the one real beauty, that each of our creations should reflect the glory of God's creation. He invoked St. Francis, "the patron of all birds, poets, and other minor nuisances."[116] Chesterton, like St. Francis, is dismissed as impractical, as a dreamer. Never mind that he keeps being proved right as a prophet. But Chesterton perhaps preferred to be known as a dreamer rather than as a prophet. After all, he said, "Men are judged by their dreams."[117]

Entering the 1930s, Chesterton was starting to look back at his career as a prolific journalist and revisiting the same issues of his early literary life and reaffirming his conclusions.

The artist who began his trade writing about art was now writing about art again: "There is nothing more dangerous than talking about Art when you are not an artist; except perhaps when you are."[118] Art, both in its form and content, was beginning to grow obscure in his youth; now it was a vast fog of nonsense. Writing, on the other hand, was going from complex to simple, or rather subtle to banal. Now it is the screaming headlines of journalism and the sky signs of advertisement. Poetry, which was fleeing in free verse, is now largely gone, and Chesterton, who said that "true art is always manual labour,"[119] wondered if the practical problem of free verse was liberality or laxity.

In the meantime, tradition, which was "the democracy of the dead,"[120] is now "the teeming vitality of the dead."[121] With the breakup of the modern world, there is one of those traditions that will "stand out stark and strong as it did before the beginning of history"[122]—the family. Chesterton warned about what was going to happen if we found ourselves living in a society that had lost its balance, "in which what was abnormal may have become normal; nay, in which the bad may become good and the good abnormal."[123] Chesterton, the great defender of Christendom, said that there was only one thing for Christians to do if their society is no longer Christian: "Launch a crusade to convert or conquer it."[124]

Western society in the early 1930s found itself fighting off the newest threats without the benefit of knowing exactly what it was defending. But even the new threats were not new. Chesterton had warned about the Prussians; then he used the same language to warn about the Nazis. He had warned about Marxism as a theory; then he warned about Soviet Communism as a reality:

> If anything is new, it is not the ideas which are supposed to belong only to this generation. It is the riots, massacres, wars, military proclamations, and wholesale executions, which were always supposed to belong especially to the past barbaric and superstitious generations. I knew all about the Communist theory of Karl Marx before I was twenty-five [1899]. What I did not know was that the Communist theory would ever make ferocious use of the Russian Secret Police, or would shoot down workmen by the score for going on strike. I had heard all about Nietzsche and the Master Mind and the reaction against democracy when I was a young art student [1892–1895]. What I did not dream of was that a mob of Master Minds would ever be able

to silence the Centrum by force and drive the Jews out of Germany. If bludgeons, bloody sabres, streets swept by artillery or rebels hanged or shot for differences of opinion—if these are new things, then I willingly agree that the situation is entirely new. But I do not see anything particularly new about the notion of a Communist State; and still less about the notion of a Dictator.[125]

There was another lurking philosophy that was not new to Chesterton, something he saw in his youth, something he repeated in *The Man Who Was Thursday* about the philosophers who hate life itself, something which was still an utter mystery to him in 1934: "The idea that life is not livable, that joy is not enjoyable, remains as utterly unmeaning to me at my present age as it did when I was sixteen years old."[126]

Chesterton's writing remained as strong as ever, just as his confidence in the truth, but as an older man, there was a slight change in his style. He had moved somewhat away from the clearly cut epigram that left no doubt, and now made more use of the rhetorical question which entreats us and encourages us not only to think for ourselves, but to think well. It was a good exercise to be questioned by G. K. Chesterton.

What I want to know is why those who are now boys, as I was then a boy, are so strangely and stubbornly twisted towards making a case against life? We also were morbid, because we were boys; we also were maniacs, because we were boys; we were quite capable of killing ourselves, because of the positive beauty of a particular woman; we also were quite capable of killing somebody else, because of the positive justice of a particular revolution. But it was always because of the positive goodness of a particular good thing. Why is it that so many people only want to make a case for the negative badness, not only of a bad thing, but of all things as being bad? The present generation has had more pleasure and enjoyment than any previous generation. Is that the right way of stating the riddle? Or is that the answer?[127]

In the essays in 1936, Chesterton was writing his last words. One gets the feeling that Chesterton knew it, too. He was saying goodbye.

What are his final thoughts for us?

He was prophetic as he always has been. He was concerned about the destruction of the family, which had come about through divorce and wage slavery, which had pulled both father and mother out of the home. But "nobody has really discussed *the alternative* to the Family. The only obvious alternative is the State.... If families will not be responsible for their own children, then officials will be responsible for other people's children."[128] The result will be that the government will gain great power over our lives, as well as interference in our lives. The most sobering prophecy: "The frightful punishment of mere sex emancipation is not anarchy but bureaucracy."[129] Think of the enforced chaos that has come about as the state has redefined marriage and family.

Chesterton worried about "the madness of machinery,"[130] and warned about a robotic world "where some horrible parody of human beings pretend to be human."[131] This is all due to the loss of tradition, the loss of custom, the literal loss of significance, of meaning. Everything is out of proportion, reflected in the world of art where "even the grotesque effects of deformity are lost in a complete loss of form."[132] Along with this is the decline in the art of controversy, where men will "make a point merely because it is part of a controversy; without worrying about whether it is a part of a philosophy."[133]

He sympathized with the revolutionary idealist "who would defy and destroy all our corrupt compromises," but he had no sympathy for the man who only used his arguments to show "his superiority to anybody he happens to dislike."[134] Most argument is opportunism. Even the right morality is preached for the wrong motives. The result is "a chaos of caprice and anarchy" that threatens "to produce a world in which men differ too much even to dispute."[135]

In Chesterton's parting wisdom to us, we can hear a weariness in his voice, but he had not given up. He still had time for literary criticism, as he devoted one essay to admitting that he had never understood what Shakespeare's poem "The Phoenix and the Turtle" was supposed to mean. And his second-to-last essay[136] was a grand tribute to his lifelong friend Edmund Clerihew Bentley, who had just published a sequel to his famous detective novel *Trent's Last Case*. When Chesterton referred to the seeming irrelevancies in the plot that turn out to be not quite so irrelevant as we had supposed, we might be reminded of the detective novel that God has written for each of us, the story of our own lives, where we think we are misled by many irrelevant things that turn out to be very relevant after all, all leading to a surprise ending. Chesterton, who made a life of seeing the meaning in everything, could look back to "those distant days" of his youth, when he dedicated *The Man Who Was Thursday* to Bentley. He could see that in spite of that novel's "melodramatic moonshine," he had the right notion of fighting against what appeared to be a world of anarchy and to resist the temptation to despair. And, thus, he finished in the light of hope.

New Witness (1912–1923)

In many ways, maybe even in most ways, the *New Witness* was a nightmare for G. K. Chesterton. It was the project of his brother

Cecil, and his brother Cecil was a project. He was a born brawler. He started arguing with Gilbert as soon as he could talk, and the argument lasted the rest of his life, but Gilbert, graciously, said they never let a quarrel interrupt a good argument. He had fierce convictions, but he had a distinct deficiency in the good humor and good-naturedness in which his brother excelled. By all accounts, he was personally likable, but none of that comes out in his writing. What he lacked in tact, he made up for in passion. He was a moral man with a sense of honor and duty and justice, but incautious to the point of destructive recklessness. He started the *New Witness*, which was a reboot of Hilaire Belloc's failed *Eye Witness*, and almost immediately found himself being sued for libel.

The accusations against G. K. Chesterton for being anti-Semitic were due in part to his association with Cecil, who used his paper to launch a full frontal attack on corrupt businessmen and politicians, many (but certainly not all) of whom were Jewish. The problem was that they were indeed corrupt, but Cecil and other writers for the *New Witness* (not GKC) emphasized their Jewishness as much as the corruption. But the Marconi Scandal (mentioned above) *was* a scandal, and *did* involve Jews, and *was* swept under the rug, and the public knew it. Gilbert knew that Cecil was the one who was wronged for pointing out what was wrong, and the guilty parties got off scot-free. But while the public forgot about it, GKC did not. He did not forget because his brother was sued for libel by one of the Jewish businessmen involved in the Marconi Scandal. To Gilbert, it made no sense that Cecil was on trial and not the Isaacs brothers. Though Godfrey and Rufus Isaacs were guilty of insider trading, Godfrey was still able to make a case that Cecil was guilty of defamation of character. Cecil could not defend himself because he had been careless and sloppy in print. In the meantime, the mess that he had made splattered onto his brother.

Gilbert had started writing for the *New Witness* as a favor to Cecil, and his column no doubt boosted the sales of the struggling paper. Liberal in its politics, conservative in its values, an open and outspoken opponent to both big government and big business, the *New Witness* also included poetry and reviews of art, literature, and theater.

When the war started, Cecil tried many times to enlist as a soldier but was rejected as being physically unfit. His body type reminded one of his brother, though on a somewhat reduced scale. However, he managed to get himself into better shape and, in 1916, he was finally accepted and went off to France to serve as a private in the light infantry. This meant that GKC would fill in as editor of the *New Witness* in Cecil's absence. In the meantime, Cecil was preparing to run for parliament. Then, after two years, and just after the war ended, the unthinkable happened: Cecil died in a military hospital in France.

Even during his time as interim editor, Gilbert moaned, "God knows I am the worst editor in the world,"[137] but he figured he could hold out until Cecil returned from the war. But Cecil did not return. It was a nightmare that Gilbert could not be woken from, and he was left holding the bag.

He had to walk a fine line, being loyal to his dead brother but avoiding the inflammatory rhetoric that got Cecil in trouble. He made changes in tone and in personnel. He no longer allowed contributions from agitating anti-Jewish writers, but he did not back off the theme of pointing out the evils of both big government and big business, both in theory and in practice. His small staff worked for a pittance, none of the writers were paid at all, the paper limped along, and he did not know how he was going to cover the cost for any of it. Under great duress, he managed to keep it afloat for another five years.

But during this whole time his own writing for the paper was consistently superb. Ironically, the essays during the war years were hardly about the war, but about history and art and literature and freedom and faith. The *Illustrated London News* essays during this same period were almost pure propaganda, while the *New Witness* essays provided the variety and wit and wonder that we would expect from a Chesterton essay.

He told funny stories about himself, such as the legendary anecdote of standing up on a bus and offering his seat to three ladies at once. "Nature has designed me along the lines of a boxing glove or a punching bag." He sparred with Shaw and Wells. "Shaw's path . . . seems to be something of a cul-de-sac."[138] Wells's problem was not that he could leave religion but that he couldn't leave it alone. "Religious belief seems to have an almost morbid attraction for those who repudiate it as unnecessary."[139]

He still enjoyed controversy. "No good was ever done by one-sided controversy."[140] And the object of controversy, he pointed out, "is conversion."[141] The enemy of controversy is not politeness or fear or even ignorance. It is apathy. "We are not divided now into those who know and those who do not know. We are divided now into those who care and those who do not care."[142]

He continued to stand up for the common man, the poor citizen who was "crushed under the weight of a colossal insignificance" and who "suffers a nightmare of being nobody."[143]

And he made fun of politicians:

"Politicians do not act; they pose."[144]

"A politician with a future means a politician with a forgotten past."[145]

"Prime Ministers could never go on strike because their work is not really needed."[146]

Electioneering is a game, a trick, and the whole trick consists of forcing people "to a choice of evils."[147] And we all know what the choice is:

In practice a conservative commonly means a man who cannot remember anything before yesterday, and a progressive means a man who cannot imagine anything beyond to-morrow. Both suffer from the unnatural narrowness of supposing that all generations led up to one generation; but for one it is the last generation and for the other the next generation.[148]

The wit is there; so is the wonder:

"Wonder . . . is the beginning of worship."[149]

"It is true that I do believe in fairy tales; in the sense that I marvel so much at what does exist that I am readier to admit what might."[150]

"Unless the sky is beautiful, nothing is beautiful. Unless the background of all things is good, it is no substitute to make the foreground better."[151]

"Nearly the chief trouble of life is that there is nothing dull in it: it is not a waste of monotony but a jungle of distractions."[152]

"In the ultimate and universal sense I am astonished at the lack of astonishment."[153]

As always he pointed out how ridiculous the latest fads were, but how even though they were fleeting they could still do permanent damage: "Nothing has contributed more to the impiety and inhumanity of our time than the exaggerated cult of cleanliness. The Pharisees had it; in the beginning they worshipped washing; and in the end they set about the slaying of God."[154]

He said we do not live in an age of faith, but an age of credulity. We do not follow eternal principles; rather, we give in to moods. Nietzsche, he warned, was a mood, a mere moment of revolt, a movement of madness, certainly not a philosophy that can be sustained.

> The narrow philosophy is that which only allows of one mood, such as rebellion, or disdain, or even despair. The large philosophy is that which allows of many moods; such as charity, or zeal, or patience. And it is so with what I count the largest of philosophies; which can be in revolt against the Prince of the World while it is loyal to the creator of the World; which can love the world like St. Francis, or renounce the world like St. Jerome. The point is that the Christian not only has mirth and indignation and compassion and comradeship and individual isolation; but he has them consistently; and each of them has a clear place in his theory of things.[155]

But he warned that the madness of Nietzsche could sweep the world away. He warned that most of the modern madness had crept into the world through the classroom because we were no longer teaching the true lessons of history, or any history at all.

> They talk a great deal about education, because it is compulsory education. Whether or no they can educate, they are always eager to compel. But as a fact their aim is the very contrary of education. It is the destruction of education, and even of experience. It is to make men forget the past, forget the facts, forget the very memories of their own lives. And if their compulsory culture spreads successfully, it is very likely that we shall be alone in knowing what was known to every man, woman and child, in the hour of our danger and deliverance.[156]

One of the main problems with state-mandated, state-sponsored, state-run schools is that the state is not accountable to parents. On the contrary, the parents are made accountable to the state. It is exactly backwards. And the philosophy conveyed in the schools, whether subtle or overt, has driven a wedge between parents and their children. Chesterton said that he heard a magistrate remark that there was a growing lawlessness in society, and it "was due to the loss of parental control." GKC instead thought that the loss of parental control was "due to the increase of official control." There was an increase of official control over parents, which was due to "the eclipse of the father by the schoolmaster."[157] Never in human history, he said, has the government had so much power over a person's life as when it started to control education. It was a fundamental shift in civilization. The fundamental thing in our society that has been undermined is the family.

> There are two human relations which modern rulers are everywhere disposed to dissolve. They are the only two relations which ordinary people are so naturally constituted as to desire. . . . A man can desire a woman as a thing of beauty, or a woman can desire a baby as a thing of beauty. And these two relations, that of man and wife or mother and child, are the only two recognized combinations founded on this natural satisfaction with the thing itself. They are also the only two recognized combinations in capitalist civilization which that system has set out to destroy. . . . It is essential to note that no other relation is really being attacked.[158]

Like a good mystery writer, Chesterton presented a conclusion that we did not see coming. He saw prophetically that there are two natural things under attack in our society today, the two primary relationships: the relationship between husband and wife, and the relationship between mother and child. Divorce, contraception, abortion, same-sex marriage are all attacks on those two relationships—husband and wife, mother and child. But the surprise is that he said they were being destroyed by our capitalist civilization. Not by our socialist civilization.

Capitalist? Yes, because that is the system that first separated the man from his wife and family by making him a wage-earner, and then separated the mother from the home by making her a wage-earner. They both work for someone else. They do not work for themselves. It was not the socialist state that did this. It was the capitalist state. Capitalism does not care about marriage. It does not care about families. It cares about the economic usefulness of individuals, first as employees and then as consumers.

But with the breakup of the family, what do you get? You get socialism.

As we noted above, Chesterton said no one ever talked about what is the alternative to the family. The alternative to the family is the state. He points out that the result of mere sex emancipation will be an increased bureaucracy. He certainly didn't trust the state as the alternative to the family. He didn't trust that "the sort of men who make our laws can be trusted to unmake our marriages."[159] It is the "maniacal idea that man owes everything to the State and nothing to the family, to the species, or to the Creator . . . a professor worshipping a policeman."[160]

We have a freer and more stable society only when we have strong families. If families fall apart, the society falls apart. But in order to have strong families, we need a political system that is based on the family, and we need an economic system that is based on the family. This is the essence of distributism. Both capitalism and socialism represent the loss of ownership. When one does not own, one is owned. Chesterton said we were becoming a race of servants. "Property has two primary social functions; it is protective and it is creative."[161] Property means ownership and independence. It has the protective function: it provides security, both against the vicissitudes of the market and the tyranny of the state. It gives a man private powers to protect him against the abuse by public powers. And it has a creative function: it builds, it produces, it makes things. It means people working for themselves, providing for themselves, ruling themselves. It means people being their own employers and their own employees. The opposite of unemployment is not employment. The opposite of unemployment is independence.[162]

What was once a strong society had fallen apart. And what did Chesterton identify as the particular point in the history of Western civilization that started the chain reaction of events that has led us to where we are now? It was the Reformation.

Let me emphasize at this point that G. K. Chesterton was one of the great ecumenical writers of the twentieth century, appealing to Catholics and non-Catholics alike. On a personal level, I know this to be a fact. He appealed to me when I was non-Catholic. So, blessed are the Protestants who take no offense at what Chesterton says about the Reformation. And this is what he says:

> I am firmly convinced that the Reformation of the sixteenth century was as near as any mortal thing can come to an unmixed evil. Even the parts of it that might appear plausible and enlightened, from a purely secular standpoint, have turned out rotten and reactionary, also from a purely secular standpoint. By substituting the Bible for the Sacrament it created a pedantic caste of those who could read, superstitiously identified with those who could think. By destroying the monks, it took social work from the poor philanthropists who chose to deny themselves, and gave it to any rich philanthropists who chose to assert themselves. By preaching individualism while preserving inequality, it produced modern capitalism. It destroyed the only League of Nations that ever had a chance; it produced the worst wars of nations that ever existed. . . . It produced the most efficient form of Protestantism, which was Prussia. It is [re]producing the worst part of paganism, which is slavery.[163]

I want to point out that Chesterton was not yet Catholic when he wrote that passage. And I also want to point out that elsewhere he sympathizes with the Reformers, whom he calls "good men who were right to be wrong,"[164] and says that the corruption in the Church was because of "bad men who had no right to their truth."[165] But ultimately the break from the Church was a break from the truth, and it began a series of errors with vast repercussions.

Protestantism is not one thing. It is many things. But one thing it does do is it keeps protesting. Protestants protest even against other Protestants. It is a form of Christianity that keeps splitting up. America has been an especially fertile ground for the birth of new Protestant sects. Chesterton does not consider them bad people: "There are individuals in all these creeds who have nothing the matter with them except their creeds."[166] But, at the same time, in America, there have arisen certain "religions of pride." And "being inspired by pride they are naturally allied to prosperity."[167] And so one kind of Protestant falls into the temptation of pride and avarice, another kind of Protestant falls into the temptation of simple rebellion, rebellion against the Church. One Protestant byproduct was Puritanism, which arose as a rival to righteousness and created the peculiarly American problem of Prohibition. Also, it "struck a sinister note of change by preserving hell and abolishing purgatory."[168]

The nature of Protestantism—to continue to protest—has led to protesting not just the Catholic Church but Christianity and even all religion. This has led to secularization, which has led to the secularization of education. Chesterton said you really cannot have a secular education because it is not even education. It does not teach the truth. On the contrary, it attacks and undermines the truth. And there can be nothing worse than doing that to children, which is exactly what is happening in the public classroom. Chesterton argued that the most effective solution to the education crisis is to take education out of the hands of the government.

But just as education cannot be conducted without religion, neither can economics be conducted without religion. Our economic system is based on a concentration of wealth, most of which is artificial because it is the trading of numbers and not even the exchange of actual goods, a giant ponzi scheme destined to collapse but built with the assumption that the government will bail it out; a system dependent on millions of wage-slaves who are in turn dependent on it; a system that measures itself by employment and unemployment, so that the unemployed think of themselves as having the right to be employed, who think only of their benefits and their retirement and of being taken care of. We expect to be fed by one industry and entertained by another. We are kept quiet by bread and circuses. The solution is not to take the present economic system and add a course or two on business ethics, and it is certainly not to put the government in charge of fixing it. Since the foundation has been destroyed, we need to rebuild civilization from the bottom up, not from the top down.

Chesterton was trying to make that argument. He was trying to *have* that argument. It was not a narrow controversy about politics. It was not about Catholic versus Protestant. It was not about details over doctrine. He said, "We have come to the end of an epoch. The heresies have burned themselves out. There is nothing but negations and the truth."[169]

> When the art of controversy comes back, it will not come from the world of sceptics and iconoclasts. It will come rather from the world of believers and of dogmatists. It will not be the work of men who merely ask questions, but of men who believe that they have

found answers. It will come out of the clash of real
convictions, which are positive and not negative; not
from those who say: "What is truth," but from those
who can still say: "This is truth"; not from Pilate but
from Paul.[170]

With revelations like this, people probably should not have
been surprised to learn that Chesterton was about to join the
Catholic Church. And it might explain why, just after he joined,
he was suddenly talking about confession. "I am not particularly
proud in believing that there is positive evil in the world. I have
no pride in it for the same reason that I have no doubt of it.
My shame and my certainty both come from the same thing;
that I have found the evil in myself."[171] He muses that psycho-
analysis is "confession without absolution, because it is without
repentance."[172]

For Chesterton's whole life, he argued for liberty. He saw
property as essential to freedom. However, "nothing is free if
the soul is not free."[173] Distributism is not a utopia. He said
that the only way to return to the Garden of Eden is the Way
of the Cross. That is not a message with wide appeal. And it
is not a popular thing to do to tell people they should not be
striving for wealth but for self-sacrifice and following Christ.
"The obligation of wealth is to chuck it. But the tale of this
very sensible test is not to be studied in the *New Witness*, but in
the New Testament."[174] In spite of its unpopularity, the truth
still "puts hooks into people, in the manner of that ancient and
magnificent metaphor which sent man forth to be the fishers of
men."[175]

But Chesterton realized he needed a new vehicle with which
to put hooks into people. He could not do it with the paper
he had inherited from his brother. He had to make the hard
decision to give it up. But he would then do something even
more difficult. He would start his very own paper.

G. K.'s Weekly (1925–1936)

G. K.'s Weekly is simply one of the most important resources for exploring the writing of one of the world's great thinkers. There are over 600 full-length essays here and nearly as many half-page essays. There are hundreds of unsigned pieces, most of which are by Chesterton. There are well over a hundred poems. Only a fraction of this material has ever been collected elsewhere. One great Chesterton devotee, Fr. Kevin Scannell, who did much to promote the writer in the 1950s and '60s, when he was fading from public sight, said that *G. K.'s Weekly* was Chesterton's real masterpiece. It was the work he put the most of himself into. He is still the affable fighter, throwing down the gauntlet with great mirth, offering challenging ideas that have never been fully addressed. "Men will not enjoy what they dare not defend."[176]

Chesterton asked his friend and fellow journalist, W. R. Titterton, to join the staff of *G. K.'s Weekly* shortly after the new paper made its first appearance. The "staff" at that point consisted of Chesterton and "Bunny" Dunham (so named because of her rabbit-like grin). Titterton said he jumped to it.

> To be with Chesterton on such a paper was like working in fairyland. Yes, he was just like a fairy godfather when he blossomed on Bunny and me in the office with gifts for good children—essays, leaders, tops-and-tails, and poems—in all his pockets.
>
> And it was fairyland when we overcrowded the Clerkenwell printing office, and Bunny, he, and I corrected proofs together, roaring (Bunny yelped) with laughter over the misprints, and sunning ourselves (Bunny and I) in his Jovian innocence.
>
> But it was equally like being at G.H.Q. Revolution. After the trivialities of the National Press, the earnestness of G.K.C. was as inspiriting as his rollick.[177]

Even though the format of *G. K.'s Weekly* seemed much the same as the *New Witness*, it was a strikingly different paper. Chesterton had immediately put his own stamp on it, both literally and figuratively, with his famous initials splashed across the banner and his infectious wit filling almost every page. But he still demonstrated that he was not a very good editor, because for nearly a year, he was writing almost the whole paper himself. But this did not seem to bother him. The thing that had once been a burden for him was now a pleasure. He said "every citizen ought to have a weekly paper of this sort to splash about in . . . every grown man ought to have this kind of scrapbook to keep him quiet."[178] This was indeed his scrapbook into which he could put anything he wanted.

His commentary on politics and culture and social issues came not only in headlines and leading articles, in long essays and short news items, but in poems and sketches and creative bits of writing that, like Chesterton himself, defied categorization. He also included fiction: short parables, but also a serialized version of what would be his final novel, *The Return of Don Quixote*. He even personally answered letters to the editor.

Along with full-length book reviews were short-short book reviews, such as this one:

> *Lenin* by Leon Trotsky. The publication of this book has caused the exile of Trotsky; but there are books equally bad written every week without any specific punishment being inflicted.[179]

The early issues are astounding for how much Chesterton material they contain, but even a writer as prolific as Chesterton could not possibly maintain this huge literary output along with his other obligations as a writer and speaker. He soon learned how to start delegating writing and editing tasks to others, and his own contributions went from several pages' worth to an average of two or three pages in each issue. Poems, essays, and articles were received from a distinguished group of writers that included Fr. Vincent McNabb, Walter de la Mare, Theodore Maynard, Ronald Knox, Maurice Baring, Shane Leslie, Charles Williams, E. C. Bentley, Eric Gill, Hilaire Belloc, Arnold Lunn, Christopher Dawson, Paul Claudel, Alfred Noyes, Ezra Pound, C. C. Martindale, and George Bernard Shaw. Even Fr. John O'Connor (aka Father Brown) wrote a piece for the paper. Famed musicologist Ernest Newman became the regular music critic. Cecil's widow, Ada Chesterton, writing under the name J. K. Prothero, was the regular theater critic. And Chesterton's wife Frances contributed an occasional poem or book review (discreetly signed "F. C."). Letters to the editor came from such notable writers as Marshall McLuhan (well before his later fame), Owen Barfield, H. G. Wells, and Dr. Oscar Levy, one of Nietzsche's first English translators. Chesterton also published the first essay by a writer named E. A. Blair, who would become better known by his pen name, George Orwell.

Like its predecessors, *G. K.'s Weekly* was always meant to be an alternative paper. Because the mainstream press, says Chesterton, has only "one great duty to the public; to prevent anything of any importance becoming public at all."[180] As an alternative paper, its highest circulation was about 8,000. Since it never had a large readership, it was never able to support itself. It relied on many benefactors, one of whom was the great orchestra and opera conductor Sir Thomas Beecham. But the main benefactor was G. K. Chesterton. Or, rather, the main benefactor was Father Brown. Whenever there was red ink at *G. K.'s Weekly*, Chesterton would write a Father Brown story and sell it to a popular magazine. So, we could say that a lot of people had to be killed in order to support *G. K.'s Weekly*. But Father Brown would always solve the murder.

Chesterton's regular column for the weekly was first called "Found Wandering" and later became "Straws in the Wind." He continued his theme of distributism, whose driving force was a genuine belief in the idea of liberty and justice for all. Liberty meant freedom with responsibility. Justice meant a just distribution of property. Property is not only the means of freedom, but it is, in a sense, the function of freedom. It gives a man something with which to do as he pleases. But property also means responsibility. It is a thing you take care of so it takes care of you. The problem with socialism is that there is no private property. The problem with capitalism is that only those with the capital have property, and they are very few in comparison with those who do not have property and capital. Chesterton wished to see property—and capital—widely distributed. Just as one man should not have all the wives, one man should not have all the property. The commandment "Thou Shall Not Steal" suggests that property is an ideal, just as "Thou Shall Not Kill" suggests that life is an ideal and "Thou Shall Not Commit Adultery" suggests that marriage is an ideal and "Thou Shall Not Bear False Witness" suggests that truth is an ideal.

But distributism was attacked from all sides as not merely impractical but crazy. In the thirteenth issue of *G. K.'s Weekly*, Chesterton responded to these criticisms: "We are called insane for attempting to return to sanity."[181] His early essays in the paper became the basis for his book *The Outline of Sanity*.

What distinguished *G. K.'s Weekly* from the *Eye Witness* and the *New Witness* was Chesterton's very positive approach to distributism as opposed to Belloc's and Cecil's negative approach, that is, their violent attacks on socialism and capitalism. Nonetheless, defending distributism meant keeping up a constant critique of both capitalism and socialism. For, according to Chesterton, "Capitalism and Socialism are very much alike, especially Capitalism."[182]

Distributism may seem like a small, specialized topic, but it involves everything. And if Chesterton had a specialty, it was everything. Everything was the thing he was always writing about, everything involved in being human.

> Our business is not so much Distributism as simply Democracy; it is not so much Democracy as simply Humanity. But in these times it needs almost superhuman fortitude to be human.[183]

The modern world is anti-human. Chesterton saw that the wholeness and dignity of human beings is under attack in a system that treats people as mere cogs in the machine, as statistics, as inconveniences. This began to happen when the modern world began to slice up humanity according to different interests, different races, different temptations. This compartmentalization of all things human is now our standard way of operating as well as educating. It is the reason why most colleges and universities cannot accommodate a complete thinker like G. K. Chesterton. He does not fit comfortably into any one department on campus; he keeps spilling over into other disciplines. They cannot handle a writer who writes about everything. He is not narrow enough. He is not specialized enough. And this is also why they cannot grasp distributism, because distributism demands an integrated way of thinking. It is dismissed because of our weakness for specialization, for the endless individual pursuits of knowing more and more about less and less. We have forgotten that a thorough knowledge of one thing must still be balanced with a general knowledge of all things.

> [This] is the chief practical result of modern practical organisation and efficiency. The division of labour has become the division of mind; and means in a new and

> sinister sense that the right hand does not know what
> the left hand doeth. In the age of universal education,
> nobody knows where anything comes from. The process
> of production has become so indirect, so multitudinous
> and so anonymous, that to trace anything to its origin is
> to enter upon a sort of detective story, or the exploration
> of a concealed crime.[184]

The result of this incomplete thinking, or lack of integrated thinking, is that the people "who dictate current opinion are governed not by principles but by obsessions, or by isolated theories."[185]

Chesterton argued that the disintegration of rational society is directly connected to a "drift from the hearth and the family."[186] The solution of course must involve a drift back. What critics of distributism have never addressed is that under the socialist or capitalist or servile systems that they defend, the family has been decimated by any number of forces, all of which directly relate to statism and commercialism, or big government and big business. Unlike the others, distributism is centered around the family and the precept that every governmental, commercial or judicial force must be dedicated to protecting, nourishing, and encouraging the family.

> Hardly anybody . . . dares to defend the family. The
> world around us has accepted a social system which
> denies the family. It will sometimes help the child in
> spite of the family; the mother in spite of the family;
> the grandfather in spite of the family. It will not help
> the family.[187]

> We live in an age of journalese, in which everything
> done inside a house is called 'drudgery' while anything
> done inside an office is called "enterprise."[188]

Chesterton saw that technological improvements that have made the world smaller have also served to make us more isolated. Case in point: the "progressive child of the twentieth century, with his earphones or his loud speaker."

> When he puts the earphones to his ears he does in fact put a mouth-gag into his mouth; as compared with the normal conversationalist conducting normal conversations. There is no harm in it, of course, in its proper place and proportion. But to fill your house, and fill your head, with voices you cannot answer, with cries you cannot return, with arguments you cannot dispute, with sentiments you cannot either applaud or denounce, is to enter into a one-sided relation and to live a lopsided life. The five senses used to be called the five wits; and to depend wholly on the receptive side of them is to be in a real sense half-witted.[189]

Astonishingly, this was written almost one hundred years ago. Besides the technological attack on the family which uses passive entertainment to separate children from their parents, there is also the technological attack to separate sex from fertility.

> Even if I did not dislike Birth-Control, I should dislike the propaganda of Birth-Control. It is not fighting out a fair battle on the high seas of the intellect; it is poisoning the wells of innocence and ignorance and simplicity. And it prevails, as all advertisement prevails, simply because there is money behind it. It is an unexpected complication in Capitalism. But the practical effect is that Liberty, Equality and Fraternity have come to mean Plutocracy, Publicity, and Pornography.[190]

> The whole business of Birth Control is quite literally a proposal to [throw] out the baby with the bath. The whole structural system of the suburban civilization is based on the case for having bathrooms and the case against having babies.[191]

Though he was describing the rise of the suburbs in England, he could just as well be describing the same thing in America. When he writes specifically about America, his observations have a pleasant sting to them:

> In the case of the laws of our American friends it may be said that they break them too easily because they make them too easily.[192]

Americans, though they claim to love freedom, actually prefer lawlessness. The modern world is the enemy of freedom. Liberty with its attendant risks is preferable to a controlled society regulated by the state and dictated by commerce. Power is in the hands of the few and most everyone else is, one way or another, dependent on those few. It is a simple matter of injustice, even if it is not a simple matter to cure the injustice.

> Men desire Peace much, but they desire Justice more; for Justice is at the root of every reason for living; nor was it only made by man.[193]

Economics must be based on the family, not on the so-called "laws" of supply and demand:

> It seems to me that since the science of economics appeared, the world has committed two enormous acts of waste. The first was throwing away a supernatural power, and the second a natural power. The first was destroying the monastic impulse and the second the parental impulse. There were certain queer people who

were ready to help men without payment, for the love of God. There were, what is still more extraordinary, people who were prepared to look after us in our hideous infancy for the love of us. Modern economy and efficiency consist in paying other people to do what these people would do for nothing.[194]

The alternative to economic freedom is economic slavery. GKC argues that the same age that tends to economic slavery "tends to social anarchy; and especially to sexual anarchy. So long as men can be driven in droves like sheep, they can be as promiscuous as sheep."[195] A fairly accurate picture of the world we see around us.

Chesterton's inspiration was Pope Leo XIII, whose encyclical *Rerum Novarum* was a foundational text for Catholic social teaching and, incidentally, distributism. But GKC certainly felt that Catholic social teaching is for the benefit of all, not just Catholics: "We are Christians and concerned with the body as well as the soul."[196]

The Distributist League, which he helped form and which elected him as its first chairman, included both Catholics and non-Catholics. Indeed, it brought together an incredibly diverse collection of individuals, who were drawn to it for its fresh approach and its compelling ideas as well as by their own dissatisfaction with the way things were and the way things were going. There was, of course, a lot of disagreement about how to bring about a more distributist society. There is no question that Chesterton was a peacekeeper as well as the unifying force in the League. This was most poignantly demonstrated by its rather rapid demise after his death in 1936. Belloc took over the editorship of the paper, which eventually changed its name to the *Weekly*. After World War II, both the paper and distributism faded away from the public arena almost completely. But with the recent revival of interest in Chesterton and his writings, people are starting to take another look at distributism as well. His arguments again sound very relevant, as big government and big business have only gotten bigger. And now more than ever, "we are putting all the best things to all the worst uses."[197]

There are some readers who enjoy Chesterton but who want nothing to do with his distributism. However, Chesterton is all of a piece. Just as you cannot separate him from his Catholicism, you cannot separate him from his ideas on Catholic social teaching. You cannot separate him from his passion for God or his passion for his neighbor. You cannot separate the two great commandments. Chesterton was dedicated to both. He gave his entire life to serving them. There was nothing wasted about the effort.

In his praise of Chesterton, his friend and fellow journalist E. C. Bentley had good reason to point out that a journalist's life is not an easy one, with the constant pressure of a deadline as well as the endless disputes with the world, but it was a life that Chesterton chose when he could have achieved relative comfort and ease and certainly fame as merely a writer of "literature."

Chesterton was once asked what advice he would give to a young journalist. He said he would tell him to write one article for the *Sporting Times* and one for the *Religious Times* and then put them in the wrong envelopes.[198] This was essentially the advice he followed himself his whole journalistic career. He wrote about religion for the secular papers. But he didn't write about religion per se. He wrote about religion when he was writing about everything else.

The Father Brown Stories

Finally, we come to the everlasting Father Brown.

In spite of all the essays and poems and books and philosophy and social criticism that flowed from his prolific pen, G. K. Chesterton is best remembered for the detective stories he wrote. And it is fitting that it should be that way, because first of all, nothing would please him more, and secondly, almost everything he wrote falls right in line with his mystery stories, achieving the same effect of presenting a puzzle to us, leading us along, and finishing us off with the shock of truth, the surprise, the revelation of things that we should already know, the solution that is utterly appropriate but entirely unexpected. It is natural that Chesterton, master of paradox, should be master of mystery, because both involve not recognizing the truth because it is strange, and then seeing what is familiar for the first time.

Chesterton changed the whole course of detective fiction when he created the character of the little priest sleuth. Previously, detective fiction had been dominated by the towering figure of Sherlock Holmes, and the main attraction of Sherlock is that he is a superhero. He knows stuff you can never hope to know. He can solve his way out of anything. We like watching bullets bounce off him. That's the whole fun of a superhero.

However, the whole charm of Father Brown is that he can solve the mysteries without the benefit of having an encyclopedia as well as an atlas and a complete run of forty-seven scientific journals inside his head. All he has is the ability to see the one thing that you missed, even though you were looking right at it.

And he has one peculiar advantage. Even though he is not a genius, it was a stroke of genius that created him: the paradox of the underdog detective. Everyone in the story and outside the story considers him outmatched. But the very thing that people think is his disadvantage is actually what gives him an edge. He's a priest. Everyone thinks he's naive. It doesn't occur to them that a guy who listens to confessions might know something about how the criminal mind works.

The inspiration for the character came when Chesterton was visiting the town of Ilkley in 1903. There he met a Catholic priest named Fr. John O'Connor, who would become one of the most important people in his life. It was Fr. O'Connor who opened Chesterton's eyes to the Catholic Faith in a way he had never considered and patiently accompanied him on the spiritual pilgrimage that would follow. He became not only a friend and a spiritual mentor but also the basis for Chesterton's greatest fictional creation, and one of the greatest characters in all of detective fiction.

It all started with a friendly conversation about an article Chesterton was proposing to write about "some rather sordid social questions of vice and crime."[199] Fr. O'Connor politely suggested that Chesterton was going in the wrong direction with his conclusion, and to demonstrate his point, the priest revealed "certain facts he knew about certain perverted practices" that jolted Chesterton, who "had not imagined that the world could hold such horrors." Later in the day Chesterton and Fr. O'Connor were talking to some Cambridge undergraduates and got involved in a very deep and lively discussion about art and philosophy. After Fr. O'Connor excused himself, the two college students expressed their admiration for the priest's keen intellect but ultimately dismissed him as no doubt being insulated and naive about the real world. Chesterton says he almost laughed out loud, for it was the priest who knew more about real evil and the real world than the two Cambridge men, who in comparison knew about as much as "two babies in the same perambulator."[200]

The incident served as the initial inspiration for a series of mysteries featuring a priest-sleuth whose strength was twofold.

One, he could solve crimes because he could get inside not only the criminal mind but the criminal heart. Two, the criminals (and everybody else) would not suspect him to suspect them because he seemed so common and naive. His twofold strength, in other words, was wisdom and innocence.

Chesterton's first collection of Father Brown stories, *The Innocence of Father Brown*, appeared in 1911. Ellery Queen called it "the miracle book of 1911." Chesterton had done something revolutionary in detective fiction, which at that time had Sherlock Holmes and his poor imitators trying to outdo one another with ever more baffling crimes and convoluted puzzles. Chesterton favored the cozy mystery, the domestic murder, with a millionaire usually performing the important service of being the murder victim and the scope of the investigation narrowed to limited time, limited space, and a limited number of suspects, with all the clues revealed to the reader as well as to the detective.

As a fan of detective fiction himself, Chesterton knew that the reader enjoyed being fooled, but being fooled fairly. A good mystery gives great pleasure when we come to the end of it and are dumbfounded by the solution. It is simultaneously humbling and gratifying to be surprised by a truth that has been sitting under our noses all along. Even though we did not expect the conclusion, we instantly recognize that it is the right one. All the clues were there, but we just didn't figure out what they all meant; suddenly they all come back to us and make sense. Even those poor souls who figure out the clues ahead of time and are not surprised by the ending are not without satisfaction; they at least have the pleasure of knowing that the author is as smart as they are. Instead of trying to imitate Arthur Conan Doyle, other writers of detective fiction soon began to imitate G. K. Chesterton.

The first Father Brown story, "The Blue Cross," remains one of the most famous and most reprinted. In it, a master criminal, the great Flambeau, pretends to be a priest and tries to steal a valuable cross. Father Brown exposes Flambeau as a fraud when the false priest attacks reason. A real priest, says Father Brown, would defend reason because "alone on earth, the Church affirms that God himself is bound by reason."[201] Apparently this idea was too shocking for Hollywood. In the film version, starring Alec Guinness as Father Brown and Peter Finch as Flambeau, the fake priest gives himself away by ordering a ham sandwich on Friday. A Seventh Day Adventist could have figured that one out.

As the series of stories continues, Chesterton introduces one of the most interesting twists in all of detective fiction: Flambeau goes from the role of archenemy to becoming a detective himself and serving as Father Brown's sidekick in the later stories. Perhaps it was a foreshadowing of the author's relationship with the real priest. It was long after Flambeau and Father Brown joined forces, after almost half of the Father Brown stories were written, that Chesterton officially joined forces with the real Father Brown. In 1922, it was Fr. John O'Connor who received G. K. Chesterton into the Catholic Church.

In *The Wisdom of Father Brown*, the second book in the series, Chesterton takes the opportunity to present a perfect satire of the super sleuth. In "The Absence of Mr. Glass," the stand-in for Sherlock Holmes is Dr. Orion Hood, who, with his brilliant methods of deduction, manages to get everything exactly and precisely and astonishingly wrong.

Cleverness is not the same thing as wisdom. Knowing a lot of facts is not the same thing as knowing the truth. In fact, as Father Brown points out in "The Duel of Dr. Hirsch," "You have to know an awful lot to be wrong on every subject—like the devil."[202] The devil, of course, is the great deceiver, and the criminals in these stories practice deception in the form of play-acting. The actor in "The Paradise of Thieves" defines an actor as "a bundle of masks." Father Brown has to unmask the masks. Chesterton got another chance to exercise his satirical gifts in "The Purple Wig," where he smashes the romantic notion of the newspaper editor. This is not a courageous, muckraking, print-the-truth-at-all-costs idealist, but rather a man whose main motivation is fear—fear of libel, fear of lost advertisements, fear of misprints, and fear of getting fired. With his blue pencil, he runs over a story, changing the word "adultery" to "impropriety" and, by mere force of habit, the word "God" to the word "circumstances." He is rightly admonished by a correspondent: "If a miracle happened in your office, you'd have to hush it up."

There is a fairly good explanation for Chesterton's exasperation with newspaper editors at this point in his life. His brother Cecil, who had exposed government corruption in high places, was suffering at the hands of those he had accused by being sued for libel, and the major newspapers suddenly went spineless. Instead of demanding justice and a full investigation of the Marconi Scandal, including the resignation of its principals, the newspapers whitewashed the central crime and clucked and fussed about minor matters.

Father Brown then disappeared for over a decade. He was forced out of retirement, as it were, due to blank necessity. He was needed in order to pay printing bills for *G. K.'s Weekly*. When he returns, we find the character has developed with the passing of time. For one thing, the humble little umbrella-toting cleric has become famous. We also learn that Father Brown is concerned for justice on a small scale and on a large scale, as he not only deals with minor complications such as murder but also is found writing a series of lectures on *Rerum Novarum*. We see him reflecting on good and evil, on his own triumphs, his own sins, and we even get to see him angry. Though the mysteries were better than ever, some reviewers suddenly complained that the stories had become too religious. What they were really complaining about was that Chesterton was now Catholic. They apparently never noticed before that the main character was a priest.

In *The Incredulity of Father Brown*, each tale contains an apparently supernatural event: a murder by a ghost or by an evil spirit or by a family curse, or, at the other extreme, a resurrection from the dead. However, the one who is expected to believe in supernatural explanations to the shocking and mysterious events is the one who doubts such explanations. It is the priest who is skeptical about the alleged miracles, while the skeptics are only too ready to believe in them. Hence, the most famous of all Chesterton's quotations: "When a man stops believing in God, he doesn't believe in nothing; he believes in anything." It comes from this book. Only it doesn't come in the neat little package that is always quoted (and always *should* be quoted). It comes from putting together two different Father Brown lines from two different stories.

In "The Oracle of the Dog," Father Brown says, "It's the first effect of not believing in God that you lose your common sense and can't see things as they are." In the very next story, "The Miracle of Moon Crescent," he tells the skeptics-turned-dupes, "You were all balanced on the very edge of belief—of belief in almost anything." (And to give credit where credit is due, it was a couple of amateur detectives, Robin Rader and Pasquale Accardo, members of the American Chesterton Society, who solved this mystery.)

Father Brown travels to America in these stories, no doubt because Chesterton traveled there himself a few years before they were written. If Chesterton ever shows any weakness as a writer, I must say it is when he writes dialogue for his American characters: they're too darn eloquent. Even allowing for the fact that Americans eighty years ago probably spoke in complete sentences, it is still difficult to believe that any average American spoke as well as Chesterton allows him to speak in these stories. On the other hand, Chesterton is quick to distinguish them from the English. The American characters have a distinctive native spirit, "a restless fire." In other words, they're all cowboys and Indians. But, in any case, American millionaires make just as good murder victims as English millionaires.

Although the priest doubts the miraculous explanations for the crimes, he never doubts the possibility of miracles. "If I want any miracles," says Father Brown, "I know where to get them."[203] It is natural to believe in the supernatural, he explains. The supernatural, of course, refers to both God and the devil. Father Brown's belief in both is always unshaken and informs both his faith and his reason. He can recognize the good man who is merely a sinner, and the bad man who wears his religion as a mask. He does not buy the false supernatural explanations for the way things happen, but neither does he buy the false scientific explanations for the way people behave: "All evil has one origin."[204]

But it is not merely belief in the supernatural that makes Father Brown think so clearly; it is belief in a creed. It is the rejection of the creed that makes the skeptics so malleable and rudderless, or, to use a word more fitting to mystery stories, *clueless*. They are all afraid, says Father Brown, of four words: "He was made Man."[205] These same four words have made a few readers uncomfortable, too. But Chesterton had the most comfortable way of making people uncomfortable. He amused them with a puzzle. He knew that every riddle wants a solution, every skeptic wants to be convinced, every criminal really wants to be caught, and every sinner wants to be forgiven.

In *The Secret of Father Brown,* we meet "The Man with Two Beards" and hear "The Song of the Flying Fish" and discover "The Worst Crime in the World." These are mysteries that look into the deepest mystery of the soul itself, exploring the nature of sin, of confession, of forgiveness. But besides that, they are rattling good yarns. In fact, the story that deals most extensively with confession is also the tale that has been called by one respected critic the best mystery story ever written—the Gothic-like "Chief Mourner of Marne."

There is one other element that sets this collection apart. It includes a prelude and a postlude, a scene of Father Brown visiting Flambeau in later years. The former thief, former detective and former sidekick of the priest has married and retired to a mountain estate in Spain. The two of them are being interviewed by an American reporter, who asks the questions we would like to ask, but doesn't get the answers we expect. The answers, of course, are the stories themselves. Full of secrets. Full of surprises.

We learn that Father Brown has a niece and that he is her guardian. We learn that he is very fond of strong Protestants because he knows they will tell the truth. We find out, not surprisingly, that he's very partial to anything that is brown. But the most intriguing revelation of all is that Father Brown makes his own startling confession about how he solved the most puzzling murders: "You see, it was I who killed all those people."[206]

The priest's methods are anything but modern; we might say anything but scientific. A criminologist attempts to get outside of the criminal and study him like a giant insect. Father Brown does just the opposite. He tries to get *inside* the criminal. "You may think a crime horrible because you could never commit it. I think it horrible because I could commit it."[207]

Understanding the motive for the crime is more important than understanding the mechanics. Understanding the motive means understanding sin. Sin destroys. It destroys from within. That is why it is horrible. It does its work in the dark. The wildest crimes, Father Brown tells us, are not the worst. It is the cold and calculated ones that are most horrifying, committed by the man who lives only for this world, who believes that his success and pleasure are the only important things, or even worse, who will do anything to save his respectability.

Most sin involves being small-minded. Forgiveness involves being large-minded, that is, generous. Father Brown points out that most of us pardon only those sins that we don't think are sins. The priest does not have that comfortable option. But Father Brown's great sympathy comes from never forgetting that he, too, is a sinner. "I don't care for spiritual powers much myself. I've got much more sympathy with spiritual weaknesses."[208]

And yet before the forgiveness is the sad discovery of the sin. In one scene, Chesterton describes his famous detective as wearily laying down his famous umbrella as a pilgrim might lay down his staff, and having "an air of some depression. . . . It was not the depression of failure, but the depression of success."[209] Solving the crime is never a pleasure for the priest. But seeing sinners forgiven is always a joy for him.

We want the criminal caught and punished, but Father Brown wants his soul to be saved. When one character protests to the priest, "But he is a convicted thief!" the little cleric gently reminds him that it was a convicted thief who is the only person "who has ever in this world heard that assurance: 'This night shalt thou be with Me in Paradise.'"[210]

According to G. K. Chesterton, every character in a novel is only the author in disguise. We certainly have evidence of this from Chesterton's own fiction. Perhaps the thinnest disguise Chesterton ever wears in the pages of a book is when he becomes Innocent Smith in *Manalive*. But one of his most ingenious masquerades is when he continually squeezes himself into the clerical costume of a little priest. The amateur detective gives Chesterton a chance to make many prophetic observations to a popular audience that might not pick up one of his other books or essays. And some of the priest's asides may sound downright *scandalous* to the modern ear. For instance, there is the scandal of democracy, the idea that all men matter: "You matter. I matter. It's the hardest thing in theology to believe....We matter to God—God only knows why."[211] Or, "You don't need any intellect to be an intellectual."[212] Or, "Materialists as a race are rather innocent and simple-minded."[213] Or, "Even the most perfectly balanced of agnostics is partially human."[214] Or, chillingly: "When a madman murders a King or a President it can't be prevented....Anybody can murder him who does not mind being a murderer."[215]

He was also amazingly prophetic about the American cult of celebrity, the rootlessness and barrenness of the university landscape, the puritanical control of society through health and hygiene, and the loudness of a few atheists who want "merely" to abolish God and the Ten Commandments.

But the device of talking through the beloved little Norfolk priest also gave Chesterton a chance to talk about...himself. He explains the dilemma he constantly faces when discussing politics with people who think there are only two sides to a political question. He reports that Father Brown, too, is drawn into political debates, "being in some sense called in on both sides."

> And as the Capitalists all reported that, to their positive knowledge, he was a Bolshevist; and as the Bolshevists all testified that he was a reactionary rigidly attached to *bourgeois* ideologies, it may be inferred that he talked a certain amount of sense without any appreciable effect on anybody.[216]

Father Brown also laments on behalf of the quotable Chesterton: "I always try to say what I mean. But everybody else means such a lot by what I say."[217]

The Scandal of Father Brown deals with all the political and religious issues that Chesterton dealt with in his writings, the same superstitions, the same sins, the same scandals. "There'd be a lot less scandal," says Father Brown, "if people did not idealize sin and pose as sinners."[218]

This final collection provides the same first-rate mysteries with marvelous plots and surprising twists, eerie crimes, and shocking solutions. Chesterton prefigured the modern medical examiners when he noted that the body is the chief witness in every murder. He picked out the most unsuspicious suspects, as in any good detective yarn, but still we don't suspect them.

Finally, there is "The Insoluble Problem," which concludes the collection on a fitting note. Although he penned a couple more stories starring his famous priest-detective, it seems there is something especially artistic about "The Insoluble Problem" being the end-piece of all the tales. The story takes place earlier in Father Brown's career and brings back his old friend, Flambeau. They encounter a case where a dead man is found hanging by the neck from a tree . . . with a sword stuck through him.

> "I was wondering," said Flambeau, "why they should hang a man by the neck till he was dead, and then take the trouble to stick him with a sword."

> "And I was wondering," said Father Brown, "why they should kill a man with a sword thrust through his heart, and then take the trouble to hang him by the neck."[219]

So, what is the solution? The title suggests there isn't one. But there is. And yet this is a mystery that ends with a mystery. Disappointed? Don't be. For the lover of detective fiction, it is a sign of hope that there is always one more conundrum to be puzzled over, one more clue to be found, one more mystery to be solved. Yes, we want the solution, but we never want a good story to end.

THE SAINT?

*"Keep before your eyes the supreme
adventure of virtue. If you are brave, think of the
man who was braver than you. If you are kind, think
of the man who was kinder than you. That is what
was meant by having a patron saint."*[1]

Most biographies tend to be about the things that happened
to a person. In the case of the saint, however, the person is the
thing that happened. The saint is holy, and the word "holy"
means "set apart." The saint is certainly someone who is set apart
from the rest of us, and the rest of us recognize it. Possibly the
first person to describe Chesterton as a saint was—this should
surprise you—George Bernard Shaw! And this was in 1921. The
double irony is that Chesterton was not yet dead—one of the
requirements for canonization—and he wasn't even Catholic,
which would also seem to be a requirement. Of course, Shaw
wasn't Catholic either. His opinion can be weighed accordingly.
But he wasn't the only one who recognized that GKC was set
apart. Within a year of Chesterton's death, several others were

saying that he was a saint: writers, friends, priests, and common folk. One of the Nicholl sisters recalled how the family maid, a young Welsh girl, reacted to Chesterton's death:

> "Oh Miss," she said, the tears in her eyes, "Oh Miss, our Mr. Chesterton dying—he was a sorter saint, Miss, wasn't he?—just to look at him when you handed him his hat made you feel sorter awesome."[2]

They were hoping that the Church would say so, too, but no movement took hold. Well, no movement even started. It was not that there was no interest; it was that there was no organized interest. It is very difficult for a layperson to get canonized. Most saints have had the advantage of being associated with an organization that is already in place, which can petition for a cause and provide support for the Church's necessary work to fully examine the candidate's life. And with a religious order, there is already a natural *cultus* in place, a group of people actively and visibly devoted to that saint and his work. It is less likely, less simple for a *cultus* to form around a layperson. And, of course, the other reason that it is more difficult for a layperson to be canonized is that it may be a greater challenge to live a holy life as a layperson. The religious life is naturally more set apart from the world. The layperson's life is necessarily "in the world." Which is why we need more lay saints. Laypeople need to see that laity is also a path to sanctification because not everyone is called to the religious life, but everyone is called to be a saint. And we need more models for that.

I believe G. K. Chesterton is a model of lay spirituality. I believe he is a model of lay mysticism. And I verily believe he is also a model of lay sanctity.

Let's consider the first two briefly, and then the third.

Chesterton says that priests are the salt of the earth. You can't live on salt but you can't live without it. He also made a priest a detective, tracking down the guilty, but not in order to condemn them, rather to pardon them. We need the priests because we need the sacraments, but the Church needs much more than the priests. The biggest part of the Church consists of those of us who sit in the pews.

A young woman in Beaconsfield was once confronted by the parish priest at St. Teresa's: "I haven't seen you at Mass for the last three weeks."

"Oh, I was there, Father. I was sitting behind Mr. Chesterton."

We have to do more than sit in the pews, of course. But it is a good idea to get behind Chesterton. He is one of the people. A married man, a working man. But he is also a misfit. A giant among dwarves. A genius among dunces. A happy man in the midst of a sorrowful world. A profound man in a shallow world. We need to be misfits in regards to the world. That is the essence of lay spirituality. This world is not our home.

Even though the Christian life is a life of prayer, Jesus reminds us to keep prayer a private thing even while we keep the rest of our lives a public thing. Fittingly, Chesterton reveals very little of his prayer life, except that he reveals all of it. He once said that he prayed that he would remember everything. God apparently granted that request, in that GKC could remember books he had read thirty years before, and not just remember them in general but quote whole passages, whole pages of them from his prodigious memory. But he didn't bother remembering unimportant things, such as where his next meeting was or when it was or other sorts of details that fill our lives and our attention. He remembered what was important. He remembered what he was really looking for. He was looking for God.

He reveals his prayer life the way it should be revealed: in his work. He reveals it in all of his writing. St. Paul tells us to pray without ceasing. Chesterton's words are a continuous act of wonder, an expression of gratitude, a cry for justice, a psalm evoking the Psalms. His evermindfulness of God is present in his work. All his books, his essays, his poems, his detective stories point to God. He is a model of lay spirituality in the way he honored his craft and his craft honored God.

He and Frances had a devotion to the Nativity, which is especially poignant, since they had no babies of their own.

> The Christ-child lay on Mary's lap,
> His hair was like a light.
> (O weary, weary were the world,
> But here is all aright.)[3]

Chesterton always had a reverence for Mary. He never had any of the Protestant objections to the Blessed Virgin, and therefore had none of those particular Protestant hurdles to his conversion. He paints a wonderful portrait of her in *The Ballad of the White Horse*, long before his conversion. It was Mary who finally brought him across the threshold of the Church. And he quietly prayed his Rosary.

He mentions Mary relatively little in his prose, but his poetry is filled with her. And some of the most mystical images in his poems involve her.

Can a layman be a mystic? Chesterton says that most people are mystics. Mysticism is common sense.

> No pure mystic ever loved mere mystery. The mystic does not bring doubts or riddles: the doubts and riddles exist already. We all feel the riddle of the earth without anyone to point it out. The mystery of life is the plainest part of it. The clouds and curtains of darkness, the confounding vapours, these are the daily weather of this world. Whatever else we have grown accustomed to, we have grown accustomed to the unaccountable. Every stone or flower is a hieroglyphic of which we

have lost the key; with every step of our lives we enter into the middle of some story which we are certain to misunderstand. The mystic is not the man who makes mysteries but the man who destroys them. The mystic is one who offers an explanation which may be true or false, but which is always comprehensible—by which I mean, not that it is *always* comprehended, but that it always can be comprehended, because there is always something to comprehend. The man whose meaning remains mysterious fails, I think, as a mystic.[4]

The mystic, says Chesterton, shows us the other side of things. The mystic is in two worlds at once, and the spiritual world with its greater reality is not obscured by the physical world with its lesser but still very important reality. Just as the mystic is in two worlds at once, so is the layman in two worlds at once. And it is important that laypeople realize they cannot live in only one world. The tendency of course is to forget the spiritual world, but there is another extreme that causes problems. There are lay movements that fail or are especially problematic because laypeople forget this world altogether. They are trying to live lives of asceticism or detachment that are suited for monks or contemplative nuns. They may succeed at being ascetics. But they fail at being laity.

What Chesterton understands and his whole life demonstrates is that there is a wholeness to holiness and a wholesomeness to holiness so that it is really possible to be in the world and not of the world. Or we could even say, at the risk of being misunderstood, it is possible to consume the world and not be consumed *by* the world.

It was Chesterton's goal to be normal. But the normal thing is to be a saint, which is what we were made to be. To be anything else is abnormal. That's the paradox.

The ordinary man has always been sane because the ordinary man has always been a mystic. He has permitted the twilight. He has always had one foot in earth and the other in fairyland. He has always left himself free to doubt his gods; but (unlike the agnostic of to-day) free also to believe in them. He has always cared more for truth than for consistency. If he saw two truths that seemed to contradict each other, he would take the two truths and the contradiction along with them. His spiritual sight is stereoscopic, like his physical sight: he sees two different pictures at once and yet sees all the better for that. Thus he has always believed that there was such a thing as fate, but such a thing as free will also. Thus he believed that children were indeed the kingdom of heaven, but nevertheless ought to be obedient to the kingdom of earth. He admired youth because it was young and age because it was not. It is exactly this balance of apparent contradictions that has been the whole buoyancy of the healthy man. The whole secret of mysticism is this: that man can understand everything by the help of what he does not understand.[5]

Chesterton said that devotion was difficult for him. He was distracted by everything. It was especially difficult in confession, where his great size was a distraction inside the cramped quarters of the confessional, and his fear that when he left he would take the confessional with him. But this could be simply his humility. His powers of concentration were astonishing. One observer said that in every conversation, no matter how the subject wandered, he had a concentration "like rhythm underneath plain chant."[6]

The thing he was concentrating on was truth. Or shall we say the One who is Truth. Chesterton seems to have been a contemplative without the benefit of the monk's cell. He was a contemplative in the midst of us, and we are privileged to know his thoughts, because he wrote them all down. One of his longtime friends, Rann Kennedy, said that Chesterton was "utterly aware of the Thing. He brought contemplation down to this earth and made it a habit. He never thought of himself. He was spitting out fire from God." Perhaps even more profoundly and mystically, Kennedy claimed that Chesterton was "fed by a perpetual Eucharist."[7]

But is this extraordinary man who claims to be ordinary, this giant, this genius, this misfit, is he a saint? In his book on St. Thomas Aquinas, Chesterton writes, "The holy man always conceals his holiness; that is the one invariable rule."[8]

It will, of course, be the decision of the Catholic Church to beatify Chesterton, but the Church does not sit around and decide, "Who should we make a saint this week?" The Vatican does not initiate the process. It all starts with a *cultus* devoted to a holy man or woman who has inspired their devotees to live a more Christly life. The *cultus* makes the case to a bishop, usually the bishop from the diocese where the subject lived. The bishop appoints a priest to conduct an investigation as to whether or not there are grounds for opening a Cause. After reading the investigator's report, the bishop then approaches the Congregation for the Causes of Saints who determines if there are any obstacles, from the Congregation's point of view, to a Cause being opened. If the Congregation has no objection, the bishop may then choose to open the Cause and the candidate will be declared a "servant of God." Then the real work begins. A postulator is appointed and the candidate's life is thoroughly examined for evidence of heroic virtue and the effect of his holiness on others then and now. Finally, the candidate would be declared Venerable. The next vote, as they say, comes from Heaven. Evidence of intercession. A miracle. That's the last step.

By the way, there is no longer a devil's advocate. People who don't know anything about the Catholic Church think they know everything about the Catholic Church. Thus, when the news that the Bishop of Northampton had announced that he was appointing an investigator for G. K. Chesterton, there were several smug critics who offered their services as devil's advocate. Besides revealing their ignorance of the process, they also tipped their hand that they felt it their duty to work on behalf of the devil. They were offering to make quick work of the three-hundred-pound, cigar-smoking journalist. A drunk. A Jew-hater. A racist. And . . . we already mentioned the smoking. But did we bring up the bit about him not wanting women to have the vote? The Catholic Church, you know, wants to bring us back to the Dark Ages.

G. K. Chesterton said that traveling narrows the mind. Some might consider this a paradox. They would be right. Those who consider it a mere contradiction do not consider that the farmer in his field thinks about more universal things than the tourist in his trains and taxis, who is focused only on getting to the next sight to see and in the meantime misses everything worth seeing. The modern man is mostly a tourist. He only sees what he comes to see.

Similarly, Chesterton also said that the most universal writers are also the most local, and like other universal writers, Chesterton also transcends his time and place by talking about his time and place. He understands that the modern world is a gigantic distraction from reality, from truth; that the fads, the fashions that seem so urgent and important, are quickly gone. Chesterton traveled the world in order to defend his front door and his back garden. The local thing is the universal thing.

And he pointed out as well that the most universal saints are also the most local. Their very names are associated with a place. Francis of Assisi, Anthony of Padua, Catherine of Siena.

Chesterton's cult, however, has turned out to be as local as the whole world. We are confronted with a contradiction. He is the patron of paradox. And he points out that sometimes the age is converted by the saint who contradicts it most. Chesterton has not only contradicted the age, he has done much to convert the age. The list includes some famous converts from a previous generation: Msgr. Ronald Knox, social critic Marshall McLuhan, actor Alec Guinness, historian Christopher Dawson, journalist Malcolm Muggeridge, writer and skier Arnold Lunn, philosophers Elizabeth Anscombe and Aurel Kolnai, novelists Evelyn Waugh, Graham Greene, Sigrid Undset and Frances Parkinson Keyes, poets Alice Meynell, Theodore Maynard and Alfred Noyes, E. F. Schumacher of *Small Is Beautiful* fame, and John Moody, founder of the *Wall Street Journal.*

In our time, we find on the list such names as prolific biographer Joseph Pearce, philosopher Peter Kreeft, scholar Thomas Howard, *First Things* editor David Mills, television host Laura Ingraham, writer Stratford Caldecott, actor Kevin O'Brien, apologist Mark Shea, science fiction writer John C. Wright, *New York Times* columnist Ross Douthat, Notre Dame theologian David Fagerberg, children's author Regina Doman, Bishop James Conley, pro-life activist Lila Rose, movie producer Jason Jones, best-selling novelist Dean Koontz, *Chronicles* editor Thomas Fleming, former President of the Evangelical Theological Society Francis Beckwith, author and psychologist Kevin Vost, and Fr. Dwight Longenecker. Plus, there are names you've never heard of whose stories are dramatic, people who found a friend in Chesterton, who helped them recover from divorce, abortion, homosexuality. One man came out of the occult. A woman from Spain told me, "Chesterton saved my life." Some came to the Church because of his writings on distributism. Some because of the book on Charles Dickens. Different books did it. For some, one quotation did it. There are hundreds of names on the list, and it features an amazing variety from all walks of life, all disciplines, all different denominations. The list of converts includes former Muslims, Mormons, and, yes, Jews. I'm on the list, too.

There is another name that goes on a different list. C. S. Lewis. Although he never became Catholic, his road from Atheism to Christianity was paved greatly by G. K. Chesterton. And it was because C. S. Lewis did not become a Catholic that so many other people did. They started reading Lewis, Lewis led them to Chesterton, and Chesterton led them to the Catholic Church. Lewis warned that reading Chesterton was dangerous. One cannot be too careful.

Chesterton points to the Truth, and he points people to the Truth, but he does it with more than just good arguments. He is more than just a good shot. "If a man were to shoot his grandmother at range of five hundred yards, I should call him a good shot but not necessarily a good man."[9] (If you recognize that line, it's likely because C. S. Lewis borrowed it from Chesterton.)

Chesterton was a good man. He could win the intellectual arguments, yes, but what ultimately wins people over is his goodness. Indeed, it is heroic virtue that the Church looks for in evaluating sainthood. But the Church does not have to convince anyone who reads his books that Chesterton's goodness is still very present in his words. It seeps through the pages like sweet perfume.

However, he was a good shot, too. His targets were not grandmothers, but skeptics and scoffers and modernists who mock the Faith or misrepresent the Faith or water it down. He them with their own weapons. "Christianity even when watered down is hot enough to boil all modern society to rags."[10] But he also appealed to the seekers. Chesterton gave them what they were looking for. He gave them God.

He won the respect of friends and enemies alike who did not share his philosophy but were affected by his goodness and his charity. He knew how to attack bad ideas without attacking the person holding those ideas. He did it most famously in his own time with H. G. Wells, a friend who was in every other way an opponent, who was a great non-believer and a great sinner, who said that if he had any chance of getting into Heaven it would be because he was a friend of G. K. Chesterton.

Someone will say: Chesterton wasn't perfect. Such searing insight takes the breath away. How do we recover from such an unexpected blow? I have even been told that Chesterton would not have approved of his own cause for canonization. But then, I still haven't found a saint who volunteered to testify on his own behalf. Chesterton said, "A saint only means someone who really knows he is a sinner."[11] Perhaps there is even hope for the rest of us.

He is not perfect, as you say. Yet there is a completeness to him. And the definition of perfection is completeness. His life, his philosophy, his words are all of a piece. Though people try to pick and choose what they like and don't like about Chesterton, we find that all the parts are connected. There is a wholeness to his holiness. It intriguingly reflects, part for part, the completeness of Holy Scripture. Chesterton is biblical in the fullest sense.

We start with the glory of Creation. GKC gives us a profound appreciation of the origins of all things, of the creativity of God and the creativity of the artist, which is a God-like act. Creation is a story that points to the storyteller, a work of art that points to the artist. Chesterton said nature is merely what the wiser of us call Creation,[12] that nature is not our mother but our sister, since we have the same Father.[13] And most importantly, he says that Creation is augmented in every one of us, that every time a baby is born it is as if God has created a new sun and a new moon because there is a new set of eyes to behold the sun and moon.[14]

It is all good, but then the serpent enters the garden. The devil. The dragon. Sin screws everything up. But Chesterton called it the good news of Original Sin.[15] The paradox. Just as the curse contains the promise of redemption, so the dragon gives us the glory of battle. Talking about God means talking about sin. Chesterton's ongoing theme is "what's wrong with the world," and it all comes down to sin. Sin is what's wrong with the world. Surprising, except for the fact that everyone already knows it. "Men do not believe in Original Sin because they believe in the *Book of Genesis*. They are ready to believe in the *Book of Genesis*, because they already believe in Original Sin."[16]

Next in the Bible comes the Law. Order. Chesterton said he is an ordinary man because he believes in order. He defends the rules because freedom exists only within the rules. Doctrine and discipline may be walls, but they are the walls of a playground.[17] "If you break the big laws, you don't get freedom. You don't even get anarchy. You get the small laws."[18] You get the mere conventions. He urged us to break the conventions and keep the commandments.[19]

After the story of Creation, the story of the Fall, and the story of the Law comes the story of the stories. The battles, the romances, the war and the wooing, the kings and the queens. Chesterton was a storyteller on an epic scale comparable to Scripture, with similar sorts of adventures, similar dramatic gestures, and similar moral lessons. Without a moral, no story makes sense. Without a moral, no story is even a story. But history *is* a story.

Chesterton's favorite story was the mystery, which is simply the story that keeps our interest, where we can't wait to find out what happens next. There are two kinds of mystery: the first is the puzzle to be solved, and the second is the truth too large to be grasped, but not too large to be contemplated. The story of

Job embodies both. "The riddles of God are more satisfying than the solutions of man."[20]

Next comes the poetry of the Psalms, where language switches into a different gear and artfully expresses every possible emotion known to man, from exuberant overflowing joy to the depths of isolation and sorrow, from being forsaken to being forgiven. The Psalms, like all good poetry, are eternal. Chesterton was always trying to talk in poetry. It is more impressive, he said, to make our prose poetic than to make our poetry prosaic. He was always trying to reach for the ultimate, and, like the Psalmist, to ascribe to the Lord heavenly things.

> The axe falls on the wood in thuds, "God, God."
> The cry of the rook, "God," answers it
> The crack of the fire on the hearth, the voice of the
>   brook, say the same name;
> All things, dog, cat, fiddle, baby,
> Wind, breaker, sea, thunderclap
> Repeat in a thousand languages—
> God.[21]

Deep answers to deep, in the language of praise and thanksgiving:

> You say grace before meals.
> All right.
> But I say grace before the play and the opera,
> And grace before the concert and pantomime,
> And grace before I open a book,
> And grace before sketching, painting,
> Swimming, fencing, boxing, walking, playing, dancing;
> And grace before I dip the pen in the ink.[22]

Then comes the wisdom of the Proverbs. Not just good advice, but nuggets of pure truth and truth well-said. Wisdom, the Proverbs tell us, is a delight to both God and man. Chesterton's great one-liners are proverbial and repeatable, but he didn't just say these words to live by, he lived by them. Here are some Chestertonian proverbs:

"Good charity is certainly better than bad criticism."[23]

"One word that tells us what we do not know outweighs a thousand words that tell us what we do know."[24]

"A man can never really be miserable if he has known anything worth being miserable for. Sorrow and pessimism are by their natures opposite: sorrow rests upon the value of something; pessimism upon the value of nothing."[25]

"The things that men see every day are the things they never see at all."[26]

And here is wisdom for debaters from a master debater: "Disagree with Socialists if you like. Disagree with Anarchists if you like. Both habits, if exercised in moderation, are good for the health. But do not lose your temper, for this is always fatal to the generous and humane institution which we call an argument."[27]

As for Ecclesiastes, it's all about knowing what matters and what doesn't. There is vanity, and then there is the vanity of vanities: "I suppose I am as vain as other men; but if I had my life to start anew, I would rather be utterly unknown except to a few intelligent friends, than to see my name sprawled across newspapers in the particular style of the modern heroes of politics and finance and sport."[28]

Then there is the Song of Songs. Chesterton's love poetry is passionate and pure and sacramental.

> Not as mine, my soul's anointed, not as mine the rude
> and light

Easy mirth of many faces, swaggering pride of song
  and fight;
Something stranger, something sweeter, something
  waiting you afar,
Secret as your stricken senses, magic as your sorrows are.

But on this, God's harp supernal, stretched but to be
  stricken once,
Hoary time is a beginner, Life a bungler, Death a dunce.
But I will not fear to match them—no, by God, I will
  not fear,
I will learn you, I will play you and the stars stand still
  to hear.[29]

And nothing compares to the letter he wrote to Frances just
before they got married:

Gilbert Keith Chesterton . . . sees how far he has gone
wrong and how idle and wasteful and wicked he has
often been: how miserably unfitted he is for what he is
called upon to be. Let him now declare it and hereafter
for ever hold his peace.

But there are four lamps of thanksgiving always before
him. The first is for his creation out of the same earth
with such a woman as you. The second is that he has
not, with all his faults, "gone after strange women." You
cannot think how a man's self restraint is rewarded in
this. The third is that he has tried to love everything
alive: a dim preparation for loving you. And the fourth
is—but no words can express that. Here ends my
previous existence. Take it: it led me to you.[30]

Then he kept falling in love with her: "I think it is no
exaggeration to say that I never saw you in my life without
thinking that I under-rated you the time before."[31]

Next come the words of the prophets. Ronald Knox said that Chesterton was a prophet in an age of false-prophets. All prophets are. Thus saith:

1902: "We are learning to do a great many clever things . . . the next thing we are going to have to learn is not to do them."[32]

1903: "Men in a state of decadence employ professionals to fight for them, professionals to dance for them, and a professional to rule them."[33]

1904: "The heretics who defend sexual manias will never admit that they are anything but chaste."[34]

1905: "Before the Liberal idea is dead or triumphant, we shall see wars and persecutions the like of which the world has never seen."[35]

1906: "The moment men begin to say, 'Where do you draw the line?' then there is nothing before us but decay."[36]

1908: "Men who begin to fight the Church for the sake of freedom and humanity end by flinging away freedom and humanity if only they may fight the Church."[37]

1909: "You may talk of God as a metaphor or a mystification; you may water Him down with gallons of long words, or boil Him to the rags of metaphysics; and it is not merely that nobody punishes, but nobody protests. But if you speak of God as a fact, as a thing like a tiger, as a reason for changing one's conduct, then the modern world will stop you somehow if it can."[38]

1910: "Hygiene may any day enforce the pagan habit of cremation."[39]

1912: "Those who talk of 'tolerating all opinions' are very provincial bigots who are only familiar with one opinion."[40]

1913: "Each sex is trying to be both sexes at once; and the result is a confusion more untruthful than any conventions."[41]

1914: "The exception has become the rule, and that is the worst of all possible tyrannies."[42]

1916: "Marriage will be called a failure wherever it is a struggle."[43]

1920: "The obvious effect of frivolous divorce will be frivolous marriage."[44]

1920: "If the policeman regulates drinking, why should he not regulate smoking, and then sleeping, and then speaking, and then breathing?"[45]

1923: "The position we have now reached is this: starting from the State, we try to remedy the failures of all the families, all the nurseries, all the schools, all the workshops, all the secondary institutions that once had some authority of their own. Everything must ultimately be brought into the Law Courts."[46]

1925: "A vast machine using electricity, water power, petrol, and so on, might reduce the work imposed on each of us to a minimum. The machine would be our master."[47]

1926: "The next great heresy is going to be simply an attack on morality: and especially on sexual morality. . . . The madness of tomorrow is not in Moscow but much more in Manhattan."[48]

1928: "Every addition to our luxuries will mean a loss to our liberties."[49]

1929: "The whole structural system of the suburban civilization is based on the case for having bathrooms and the case against having babies."[50]

1930: "Modern materialism is solemn about sports because it has no other rites to solemnize."[51]

1932: "We are already drifting horribly near to a new war, which will probably start on the Polish border."[52]

1933: "The next war will be the most horrible of all wars."[53]

1933: "China [is] the only real rival to Christendom."[54]

1935: "There has spread over our social life a curious atmosphere of waste; perhaps best symbolized by a loudspeaker pouring torrents of music out of an empty shop into an empty street."[55]

1936: "There hovers on the horizon sweeping scourges of sterilization or social hygiene applied to everybody and imposed by nobody."[56]

His prophecies are stunning and sobering for their accuracy. But also encouraging. Every prophecy is a call for repentance and therefore a message of hope. Things do not have to end this way. It goes back to the doctrine of conditional joy. It is an affirmation of free will. Chesterton said, "The best kind of prophecy is to say, not what will occur but what should occur."[57] And, like a true prophet, he tells us not to look to the future, but to the past. As Jeremiah tells us: "Stand by the roads, and look, and ask for the ancient paths, where the good way is; and walk in it, and find rest for your souls" (Jer 6:16). Chesterton offers a corollary about what happens if we do not ask for the ancient path, if we do not look for where the good way is: "If you forget the far-off things, your sons and grandsons will remember them and rise up against you."[58]

Then comes the evangelist, the bringer of the Good News. Chesterton begins by taking on the textual critics and the revisionists: "State first of all what Jesus said, not what you think He would have said if He had expressed Himself more clearly."[59]

The world cannot accept the Good News, he says, because they think it is too good to be true. We cannot cope with the freedom of God, which is the miraculous, and the freedom of man, which is responsibility. We cannot cope with a God who is able to let himself die, and a man who is able to rise from the dead.

On the third day, the friends of Christ coming at daybreak to the place found the grave empty and the stone rolled away. In varying ways they realized the new wonder; but even they hardly realized that the world had died in the night. What they were looking at was the first day of a new creation, with a new Heaven and a new earth; and in a semblance of the gardener God walked again in the garden, in the cool not of the evening but the dawn.[60]

This is the story that is different from any other. Chesterton says that the religion of the world is not divided into "fine shades of mysticism" or other divisions according to the development of historical and philosophical ideas about the divine. It is divided between those who are bringing the message of the Gospel and those who have not yet heard it, or cannot yet believe it.[61]

Then, the apostle. Chesterton's essays are letters to the world, epistles of common sense. St. Paul says, in a Chesterton-like paradox: "When I am weak, then I am strong" (2 Cor 12:10). GKC in a similar exhortation says: "The one perfectly divine thing, the one glimpse of God's paradise given on earth, is to fight a losing battle—and not lose it."[62] His precepts also drop like the pearls from Paul. More words to live by, chapter and verse:

> "Drink because you are happy, but never because you are miserable."[63]

> "Do not forget the real God or the real world."[64]

> "What are we to do? Keep our tempers, primarily. And after that, look the situation in the face, and think."[65]

> "Let us love mercy and walk humbly."[66]

Finally, another great mystery: the end of the world. Chesterton tells us, first of all, that we must not suppose that the end of our own age is the end of the world, simply because it is the end of us. But secondly, he tells us that there really *is* an end of the world in that the world has an aim, an ultimate purpose. And thirdly, and finally, there is a finally. There *will* be an end of the world. "The end of the world is more actual than the world it ends."[67] It could be near, it could be far. "Man may stand on the earth generation after generation, and yet each birth be his positively last appearance."[68] At the end of the world we will not only finally face God, we will really face each other.

> We follow the feet
> Where all souls meet
> In the inn at the end of the world.[69]

Chesterton says the Catholic Church is a playground.[70] He also says Heaven is a playground.[71] There should certainly be that sort of continuity.

The path to sainthood leads through beatification. It would do us well to point out the beatitudes: Blessed are the poor in spirit, blessed are those who mourn, blessed are the meek, blessed are those who hunger and thirst for righteousness, blessed are the merciful, blessed are the pure in heart, blessed are the peacemakers, blessed are those who are persecuted for the sake of righteousness. These are all descriptions of G. K. Chesterton. It is not difficult at all to make the case that he epitomizes each of the beatitudes with his humility, his sympathy, his kindness, his thirst for justice, his charity to his enemies, his purity and goodness, and his patience with those who attacked him, but he also gave his own flavor to blessedness: "Blessed is he that expecteth nothing, for he shall be gloriously surprised."[72]

One of his fellow journalists, William Titterton, wrote the first biography of Chesterton, and in the conclusion expressed the hope that the Church would make Chesterton a saint: "He was always thinking about God."[73] Another journalist, J. C. Squire, said that Chesterton "constantly sees the eternal behind the temporal." And the saintly Fr. Vincent McNabb said:

> It was hard to speak with Gilbert Chesterton and not to think—and think of God. Even the atheist who spoke with him, and who would have despised the God of Abraham, the God of Isaac, the God of Jacob, felt he would like to know about the God of Gilbert Chesterton—this God whom the very laughter of Gilbert Chesterton seemed to prove was such a lovably human, though transcendent being...[74]

Theodore Maynard was a poet and essayist who contributed pieces to both the *New Witness* and *G. K.'s Weekly*. He said that Chesterton "more than any other man has moulded my life." A Catholic convert through Chesterton's (and distributism's) influence, Maynard also said that GKC "was one of the worst editors in the history of journalism," but he tempers that assessment with: "No one . . . can for a moment suspect me of a wish to belittle a man whom I shall always look upon not only as the most luminous intelligence I have ever encountered but also as a saint."[75]

May Bateman visited Top Meadow in 1927 in order to write about the house. She described it as "Chestertonian" and then ended up writing more about its owner and chief occupant. She described him as "a conventional knight in shining armor, climbing up a steep and narrow track, beset with dragons and fearsome Apocryphal beasts with fiery tongues and glittering scales... who did not even know the monsters were around him because his eyes were so firmly fixed on his goal in the sky."[76]

She sees him walk through Beaconsfield followed by beggars. "The light before him never blinds him to the presence by the roadside of a fellow creature who might need his help; but it does take him forward without notice of the worldly cares which beset most of humanity."[77]

She continues:

> He is . . . amazingly modest . . . innately humble of mind, he is a complete child in the scriptural sense of the Gospel. He is great enough to know that one must make himself very small before he can enter the gate of Heaven. Outward events cannot change him. If he were to become tomorrow the Mussolini of the British Empire, I am convinced he would be as simple-minded and as simple-hearted as he is today, as ready to autograph the book some unknown young bank clerk has sent him; to get up, however tired, to take Quoodle for a walk for no better reason than that he thought his dog seemed dull and listless; to give time and attention to some stranger who would bore another man to tears; in short, to think of others rather than of himself.

> The difference between him and most of us is that he really lives by faith. The stirring of the spirit is as necessary to him as the air he breathes. His vision is fixed and Catholicism is the essence of his being, moving and directing him by its immortal hope and its inspiration, recognized by him for what it is, the only vision that opens up on a world without end.[78]

St. Thomas More was not canonized until G. K. Chesterton's lifetime. Leading up to the canonization, Chesterton said, in 1929, that More was important because he not only defended the Church against the state, but he defended the family against the state.[79] In light of problems plaguing both the Church and the family in Chesterton's time, he said that More was more important then than he was in his own time, and he would be more important in the future than he was in Chesterton's day. I would argue that the same could be said of G. K. Chesterton. He also defended the Church against the state and defended the family against the state. And he is more important now than he was when he lived. He will be even more important in the future than he is now. But even if he will be more important in the future, I hope that it will not take the Church as long to canonize Chesterton as it did with Thomas More.

We can't help but admire him, but when we admire Chesterton and his great genius and his enormous creative talents, we are being thankful for God's gifts, God's gifts to Chesterton, God's gifts to us through Chesterton. Everything points to God. And that is what saints do: they point us to God.

BIBLIOGRAPHY

Books by Chesterton
(This is not a complete list, but includes only those books referenced in the text.)

Greybeards at Play (1900)

The Wild Knight (1900)

The Defendant (1901)

Twelve Types/Varied Types (1903)

Robert Browning (1903)

G. F. Watts (1904)

The Napoleon of Notting Hill (1904)

Heretics (1905)

Charles Dickens (1906)

The Man Who Was Thursday (1908)

Orthodoxy (1908)

George Bernard Shaw (1909)

The Ball and the Cross (1910)

What's Wrong With the World (1910)

William Blake (1910)

Appreciations and Criticisms of Charles Dickens (1911)

The Innocence of Father Brown (1911)

The Ballad of the White Horse (1911)

Manalive (1912)

The Victorian Age in Literature (1913)

Magic (1913)

The Flying Inn (1914)

The Wisdom of Father Brown (1914)

Divorce versus Democracy (1916)

A Short History of England (1917)

Utopia of Usurers (1917)

Irish Impressions (1919)

The Superstition of Divorce (1920)

The New Jerusalem (1920)

Eugenics and Other Evils (1922)

What I Saw in America (1922)

The Ballad of St. Barbara (1922)

St. Francis of Assisi (1923)

The Everlasting Man (1925)

William Cobbett (1925)

The Incredulity of Father Brown (1926)

The Outline of Sanity (1926)

The Queen of Seven Swords (1926)

The Catholic Church and Conversion (1927)

The Return of Don Quixote (1927)

The Secret of Father Brown (1927)

The Judgment of Dr. Johnson (1927)

Culture and the Coming Peril (1927)

Robert Louis Stevenson (1927)

The Thing (1929)

G.K.C. as M.C. (1929)

The Poet and the Lunatics (1929)

The Resurrection of Rome (1930)

Chaucer (1932)

Sidelights on New London and Newer York (1932)

Christendom in Dublin (1932)

St. Thomas Aquinas (1933)

The Scandal of Father Brown (1935)

The Well and the Shallows (1935)

The Way of the Cross (1935)

Autobiography (1936)

The Coloured Lands (1938)

The End of the Armistice (1940)

The Common Man (1950)

The Surprise (1952)

A Handful of Authors (1953)

The Spice of Life (1964)

Time's Abstract and Brief Chronicle (in Collected Works, Vol. 11, 1989)

Where All Roads Lead (in Collected Works, Vol. 3, 1990)

Collected Poetry (Collected Works, Vol. 10, Parts I–III, 1994–2010)

Basil Howe (2001)

The Soul of Wit: G. K. Chesterton on William Shakespeare (2012)

Periodicals with Essays by Chesterton

(As above, this list includes only those periodicals referenced in the text.)

The Debater (1891–1893)

The Speaker (1892–1906)

Daily News (1901–1913)

Illustrated London News (1905–1936, reprinted in the Collected Works, Vols. 27–36)

The Albany Review (1907)

T.P.'s Weekly (1910, 1926)

Eye Witness (1911–1912)

New Witness (1912– 1923)

G. K.'s Weekly (1925–1936)

New York American (1931–1935)

The Listener (1932–1936)

Chesterton Review (1974–2017)

Periodicals with References to Chesterton

(Reports of speeches, personal accounts, etc.)

London Evening News (July 6, 1915)

The Tablet (November 8, 1919)

Philadelphia Evening Public Ledger (February 18, 1921)

Boston Globe, (January 13, 1921)

Nashville Tennessean (March 23, 1921)

Hastings Observer (March 21, 1925)

Extension Magazine (January 1927)

The Observer (July 3, 1927)

Dundee Courier (January 13, 1928)

Yorkshire Post (September 29, 1929; May 10, 1930; June 16, 1936)

Western Morning News and Mercury (October 9, 1929)

Seattle Times (March 10, 1931)

Lincolnshire Echo (October 28, 1932)

Plymouth and Exeter Gazette (June 19, 1936)

Catholic Herald (June 19, 1936)

Aberdeen Journal (June 1, 1939)

Manchester Guardian (November 15, 1924; October 31, 1932; 1955; et al)

Sign (February 1943)

The Nineteenth Century and After (1946)

Heritage Magazine (January 1956)

Books about Chesterton

Dale Ahlquist, *G. K. Chesterton: The Apostle of Common Sense* (2003, Ignatius)

–, *Common Sense 101: Lessons from G. K. Chesterton* (2006, Ignatius)

–, *The Complete Thinker: The Marvelous Mind of G. K. Chesterton* (2012, Ignatius)

John Beaumont, *Roads to Rome: A Guide to Notable Converts from Britain and Ireland from the Reformation to the Present Day* (2010, St. Augustine's Press)

–, *The Mississippi Flows into the Tiber: A Guide to Notable American Converts to the Catholic Church* (2014, Fidelity Press)

E. C. Bentley, *Those Days* (1940, Constable and Co.)

–, (Introduction) *Selected Essays of G. K. Chesterton* (1949, Methuen)

–, et al, *The First Clerihews* (1982, Oxford University Press)

Patrick Braybrooke, *Gilbert Keith Chesterton* (1972, Chelsea Publishing Co.)

Nancy Carpentier Brown, *The Woman Who Was Chesterton* (2015, ACS Books)

Émile Cammaerts, *The Laughing Prophet* (1937, Methuen)

Cecil Chesterton, *G. K. Chesterton: A Criticism* (1908, Alston Rivers)

R. A. Christophers, ed., *The British Library Catalogue of Additions to the Manuscripts: The G. K. Chesterton Papers* (2001, The British Library)

Cyril Clemens, *Chesterton as Seen by His Contemporaries* (1972, Gordon Press)

Denis J. Conlon, *G. K. Chesterton: A Reappraisal* (2015, Methuen)

–, ed., *G. K. Chesterton: The Critical Judgments* (1976, Antwerp Studies in English Literature)

–, ed., *G. K. Chesterton: A Half-Century of Views* (1987, Oxford University Press)

Gerald Cumberland, *Set Down in Malice: A Book of Reminiscences* (1919, Brentano's)

Bernard Falk, *He Laughed in Fleet Street* (1933, Hutchinson)

Ann Farmer, *Chesterton and the Jews: Friend, Critic, Defender* (2015, Angelico Press)

Spencer Howe, *G. K. Chesterton, Italy, and the Church: Conversion and Reception* (2014, STL Dissertation, Lateran Pontifical University)

Ian Hunter, *Nothing to Repent, a Life of Hesketh Pearson* (1987, Hamish Hamilton)

Ian Ker, *G. K. Chesterton: A Life* (2011, Oxford University Press)

Theodore Maynard, *The World I Saw* (1938, Bruce Publishing Co.)

Beverley Nichols, *25: Being a Young Man's Recollections of His Elders and Betters* (1935, Penguin)

Alfred Noyes, *Two Worlds for Memory* (1953, Lippincott)

Francis E. Nugent, ed., *A Vincent McNabb Anthology* (1955, Blackfriars)

William Oddie, *Chesterton and the Romance of Orthodoxy: The Making of GKC 1874–1908* (2008, Oxford University Press)

–, ed. *The Holiness of G.K. Chesterton* (2010, Gracewing)

Joseph Pearce, *Wisdom and Innocence: A Life of G. K. Chesterton* (1996, Ignatius)

–, *Literary Converts* (1999, Ignatius)

Maurice Reckitt, *As It Happened: An Autobiography* (1941, J.M. Dent)

Brocard Sewell, *Cecil Chesterton* (1975, St. Albert's Press)

–, *G. K.'s Weekly: An Appraisal* (1990, The Aylesford Press)

–, *My Dear Time's Waste* (1966, St. Albert's Press)

John Sullivan, ed., *G. K. Chesterton: A Centenary Appraisal* (1974, Harper and Row)

W. R. Titterton, *G. K. Chesterton: A Portrait* (1936, Alexander Ouseley Limited)

–, *The World Is So Full* (1961, privately printed)

Maisie Ward, *Gilbert Keith Chesterton* (1943, Sheed and Ward)

–, *Return to Chesterton* (1952, Sheed and Ward)

–, *Unfinished Business* (1964, Sheed and Ward)

Unpublished Documents

Thomas Derrick, Letter to Maisie Ward, 1955, No. 73195, G. K. Chesterton Papers, British Library Archives, University of Notre Dame, South Bend, Indiana

Author's notes from personal interviews of first and secondhand accounts of undocumented events

NOTES

Introduction
1 "The Unfinished Temple," *What's Wrong with the World*
2 *Illustrated London News*, July 16, 1910
3 "The Five Deaths of the Faith," *The Everlasting Man*
4 "Rome via Jerusalem," *Gilbert Keith Chesterton* (Maisie Ward)
5 "The Eternal Revolution," *Orthodoxy*
6 "The Rebellion of the Rich," *A Short History of England*
7 "The New Hypocrite," *What's Wrong with the World*
8 *Illustrated London News*, December 16, 1911
9 "The Remarkable Mr. Turnbull," *The Napoleon of Notting Hill*
10 *Illustrated London News*, May 30, 1908
11 *Daily News*, July 1, 1911
12 *Daily News*, April 28, 1906
13 *Illustrated London News*, March 4, 1916
14 "The Moral Philosophy of Meredith," *A Handful of Authors*
15 *Illustrated London News*, January 13, 1912
16 "The New Groove," *The Common Man*
17 *Illustrated London News*, June 19, 1915
18 *Illustrated London News*, March 25, 1911
19 *Daily News*, January 8, 1908

The Man
1 *Illustrated London News*, October 31, 1925
2 "The Convert," *Collected Poetry* (CW V. 10 pt. III)
3 "The Three Orders," *St. Francis of Assisi*
4 "Creation Day," *Collected Poetry* (CW V. 10 pt. I)
5 "The Ballad of St. Barbara," *Collected Poetry* (CW V. 10 pt. III)
6 "The Meaning of the Crusade," *The New Jerusalem*
7 Letter from Belloc to Father O' Connor, August 23, 1922
8 "The God with the Golden Key," *Autobiography*
9 "At School with G.K.C.," *Those Days* (Bentley)
10 *Daily News*, February 20, 1904

11 "They Are All Puritans," *Sidelights*

12 *Illustrated London News*, July 13, 1929

13 *Illustrated London News*, April 20, 1907

14 *Illustrated London News,* November 21, 1914

15 "Omar and the Sacred Vine," *Heretics*

16 *Illustrated London News*, April 20, 1907

17 *Extension Magazine*, January 1927

18 *Chicago Daily Tribune*, February 23, 1921

19 Ibid.

20 Ibid.

21 "The Banner of Beacon," *Manalive*

22 "To Frances," *Gilbert Keith Chesterton* (Maisie Ward)

23 "The Irishman," *George Bernard Shaw*

24 *G. F. Watts*

25 "How to Be a Lunatic," *Autobiography*

26 *The Listener,* March 18 1936

27 "Nationality and the French Wars," *A Short History of England*

28 "God and Comparative Religion," *The Everlasting Man*

29 "The Backward Bolshie," *The Well and the Shallows*

30 *Chesterton Review*, V. IV, N. 2, Spring–Summer, 1978

31 *New Witness*, June 18, 1914

32 *The Spectator*, June 19, 1936

33 "Prohibition in Fact and Fancy," *What I Saw in America*

34 *New Witness*, September 30, 1915

35 "The Flag of the World," *Orthodoxy*

36 "The Great Victorian Poets," *The Victorian Age in Literature*

37 "Books for Boys," *The Common Man*

38 "The Notebook," *Gilbert Keith Chesterton* (Maisie Ward)

39 "The Flag of the World," *Orthodoxy*

40 "How to Be a Lunatic," *Autobiography*

41 *T. P.'s and Cassell's Weekly*, January 23, 1926

42 Ibid.

43 Ibid.

44 Ibid.

45 Ibid.

46 "The Fantastic Suburb," *Autobiography*

47 "The Diabolist," *Tremendous Trifles*
48 "The Six Philosophers," *The Man Who Was Thursday*
49 "Columbus," *Gilbert Keith Chesterton* (Maisie Ward)
50 *Illustrated London News*, January 13, 1906
51 *G.K.'s Weekly*, January 21, 1928
52 Ibid.
53 Letter from GKC circulated to the press, August 7, 1915
54 *Illustrated London News*, January 1, 1935
55 *St. Louis Post-Dispatch*, March 19, 1921
56 *Baltimore Sun*, February 4, 1921
57 *Nashville Tennessean*, March 23, 1921
58 *Boston Sunday Post*, January 16, 1921
59 *Philadelphia Evening Public Ledger*, February 18, 1921
60 *Brandon Daily Sun*, March 29, 1921
61 *Cleveland Press*, March 2, 1921
62 *New York Times*, April 13, 1921
63 *Yorkshire Post*, September 29, 1924
64 *Lincolnshire Echo*, October 28, 1932
65 *New York Times*, June 8, 1924
66 *Hastings Observer*, March 21, 1925
67 *Yorkshire Post*, June 16, 1936
68 Letter from Thomas Derrick to Maisie Ward dated April 20, 1944
69 Private correspondence
70 *G.K.'s Weekly*, November 12, 1927
71 "Chesterton," *25: Being a Young Man's Recollections of His Elders and Betters* (Nichols)
72 *Daily News,* July 18, 1908
73 *Daily News*, October 7, 1905
74 *Sign*, February 1943
75 "Rome via Jerusalem," *Gilbert Keith Chesterton* (Maisie Ward)
76 "Serious but Never Solemn," *Return to Chesterton* (Maisie Ward)
77 *G.K.'s Weekly*, January 3, 1935
78 "The Exception Proves the Rule," *The Catholic Church and Conversion*
79 "The Book of Job," *G.K.C. as M.C.*

80   *Illustrated London News*, January 17, 1914

81   *Daily News*, February 24, 1912

82   "The Gloomy Dean," *Gilbert!* March–April, 2014

83   Ibid.

84   *Literary Digest*, September 23, 1922

85   Ibid.

86   *Tablet*, August 19, 1922

87   "Serious but Never Solemn," *Return to Chesterton* (Maisie Ward)

88   "The Usual Article," *The Thing*

89   *Toronto Daily Star*, October 4, 1922

90   "Silver Wedding," *Gilbert Keith Chesterton* (Maisie Ward)

91   "Apologia," *G.K.C. as M.C.*

92   *G.K.'s Weekly*, April 24, 1926

93   "The Return of the Romans," *The Resurrection of Rome*

94   *G.K.'s Weekly*, May 29, 1926

95   "The Holy Island," *The Resurrection of Rome*

96   Ibid.

97   Ibid.

98   "The Pillar of the Lateran," *The Resurrection of Rome*

99   "The Rolling Roads," *G.K. Chesterton: A Reappraisal* (Conlon)

100 "Columbus," *Gilbert Keith Chesterton* (Maisie Ward)

101 All quotations from the lectures are from the Archives of the University of Notre Dame.

102 *Bradford Era*, December 20, 1930

103 *Olean Times*, November 28, 1930

104 An account of the debate can be found in my book *Common Sense 101: Lessons from G.K. Chesterton*

105 University of London, June 28, 1927

106 *Berkeley Daily Gazette*, March 6, 1931

107 *Seattle Times*, March 11, 1931

108 Personal interview with former producer from BBC Radio

109 *Manchester Guardian*, November 1, 1932

110 "Why Didn't G.K. Chesterton Ever Win a Nobel Prize?" *Gilbert!* April–May, 2004

111 *Yorkshire Post*, May 10, 1930

112 "Last Days," *Gilbert Keith Chesterton* (Maisie Ward)

113 *William Blake*

The Writer

1   *The Observer*, February 26, 1911
2   *Illustrated London News*, August 17, 1929
3   "The Paradoxes of Christianity," *Orthodoxy*
4   This famous line is not actually from the book, but was one that Chesterton made in more than one speech. One source is the Chesterton Memorial Number of the *Mark Twain Quarterly*, Spring, 1937
5   "The Unfinished Temple," *What's Wrong with the World*
6   "Folly and Female Education," *What's Wrong with the World*
7   "The Testament of St. Francis," *St. Francis of Assisi*
8   "Francis the Builder," *St. Francis of Assisi*
9   "Le Jongleur de Dieu," *St. Francis of Assisi*
10 Ibid.
11 Ibid.
12 "The Mirror of Christ," *St. Francis of Assisi*
13 "Le Jongleur de Dieu," *St. Francis of Assisi*
14 Ibid.
15 "On Two Friars," *St. Thomas Aquinas*
16 Ibid.
17 Ibid.
18 Ibid.
19 "A Meditation on the Manichees," *St. Thomas Aquinas*
20 "On Two Friars," *St. Thomas Aquinas*
21 "A Meditation on the Manichees," *St. Thomas Aquinas*
22 "God and Comparative Religion," *The Everlasting Man*
23 "The God in the Cave," *The Everlasting Man*
24 "The Riddles of the Gospel," *The Everlasting Man*
25 "The Strangest Story in the World," *The Everlasting Man*
26 "The Five Deaths of the Faith," *The Everlasting Man*
27 *The Observer*, July 3, 1927
28 "The Vision of the King," *The Ballad of the White Horse*
29 "The Scouring of the Horse," *The Ballad of the White Horse*
30 *Daily News*, May 21, 1901
31 *Daily News*, August 7, 1901
32 Ibid.
33 *Daily News*, August 30, 1901

34 *Daily News*, March 14, 1903
35 Ibid.
36 *Daily News* May 30, 1903
37 *Daily News*, May 7, 1904
38 Ibid.
39 *Daily News*, January 13, 1906
40 *Daily News*, July 6, 1907
41 *Daily News*, November 28, 1908
42 Ibid.
43 *Daily News*, May 30, 1908
44 *Daily News*, May 23, 1908
45 *Daily News*, October 17, 1908
46 *Daily News*, September 19, 1908
47 *Daily News*, February 25, 1911
48 *Daily News*, February 19, 1910
49 *Daily News*, February 25, 1911
50 *Daily News*, February 1, 1913
51 *Daily News*, April 20, 1912
52 *Daily News*, January 25, 1913
53 *Illustrated London News*, December 8, 1906
54 *Illustrated London News*, December 22, 1906
55 *Illustrated London News*, October 6, 1906
56 Ibid.
57 *Illustrated London News*, January 4, 1908
58 *Illustrated London News*, April 24, 1909
59 *Illustrated London News*, June 12, 1909
60 *Illustrated London News*, October 31, 1908
61 *Illustrated London News*, April 3, 1909
62 *Illustrated London News*, August 7, 1909
63 *Illustrated London News*, November 7, 1908
64 *Illustrated London News*, June 1, 1912
65 *Illustrated London News*, January 20, 1912
66 *Illustrated London News*, June 1, 1912
67 *Illustrated London News*, March 9, 1912
68 *Illustrated London News*, February 10, 1912
69 *Illustrated London News*, January 27, 1912
70 Ibid.

71 *Illustrated London News*, June 22, 1912
72 *Illustrated London News*, May 27, 1911
73 *Illustrated London News*, July 29, 1911
74 *Illustrated London News*, May 22, 1915
75 *Illustrated London News*, October 17, 1914
76 *Illustrated London News*, July 24, 1915
77 *Illustrated London News*, April 21, 1917
78 *Illustrated London News*, January 6, 1917
79 *Illustrated London News*, September 29, 1917
80 *Illustrated London News*, February 24, 1917
81 *Illustrated London News*, March 17, 1917
82 *Illustrated London News*, February 3, 1917
83 Ibid.
84 *Illustrated London News*, March 30, 1918
85 *Illustrated London News*, May 20, 1922
86 *Illustrated London News*, April 1, 1922
87 Ibid.
88 *Illustrated London News*, June 3, 1922
89 Ibid.
90 *Illustrated London News*, June 24, 1922
91 Ibid.
92 *Illustrated London News*, December 9, 1922
93 *Illustrated London News*, February 10, 1923
94 *Illustrated London News*, June 9, 1923
95 Ibid.
96 Ibid.
97 Ibid.
98 *Illustrated London News*, June 30, 1923
99 *Illustrated London News*, November 15, 1924
100 *Illustrated London News*, November 29, 1924
101 *Illustrated London News*, October 11, 1924
102 *Illustrated London News*, August 25, 1928
103 *Illustrated London News*, March 19, 1927
104 *Illustrated London News*, October 9, 1926
105 *Illustrated London News*, February 25, 1928
106 *Illustrated London News*, August 4, 1928
107 *Illustrated London News*, September 1, 1928

108 *Illustrated London News*, September 8, 1928
109 *Illustrated London News*, June 12, 1926
110 *Illustrated London News*, January 28, 1928
111 *Illustrated London News*, March 3, 1928
112 *Illustrated London News*, March 31, 1928
113 *Illustrated London News*, February 11, 1928
114 *Illustrated London News*, March 23, 1929
115 *Illustrated London News*, May 11, 1929
116 *Illustrated London News*, July 18, 1931
117 *Illustrated London News*, June 8, 1929
118 *Illustrated London News*, January 13, 1934
119 *Illustrated London News*, March 8, 1934
120 "The Ethics of Elfland," *Orthodoxy*
121 *Illustrated London News*, July 1, 1933
122 *Illustrated London News*, June 17, 1933
123 *Illustrated London News*, February 17, 1934
124 Ibid.
125 *Illustrated London News*, April 7, 1934
126 *Illustrated London News*, June 24, 1933
127 *Illustrated London News*, February 18, 1933
128 *Illustrated London News*, January 4, 1936
129 Ibid.
130 *Illustrated London News*, April 11, 1936
131 *Illustrated London News*, December 21, 1935
132 *Illustrated London News*, June 20, 1936
133 *Illustrated London News*, May 2, 1936
134 Ibid.
135 Ibid.
136 *Illustrated London News*, June 13, 1936
137 *New Witness*, December 7, 1916
138 *New Witness*, April 26, 1917
139 *New Witness*, May 10, 1918
140 *New Witness*, August 2, 1918
141 *New Witness*, December 31, 1920
142 *New Witness*, December 20, 1918
143 *New Witness*, August 2, 1917
144 *New Witness*, August 2, 1918

145 *New Witness*, January 28, 1920
146 *New Witness*, August 30, 1918
147 *New Witness*, January 10, 1919
148 *New Witness*, May 14, 1920
149 *New Witness*, April 6, 1916
150 *New Witness*, June 15, 1916
151 *New Witness*, October 12, 1916
152 *New Witness*, December 7, 1916
153 *New Witness*, January 25, 1917
154 *New Witness*, September 2, 1915
155 *New Witness*, October 15, 1920
156 *New Witness*, September 24, 1920
157 *New Witness*, October 21, 1921
158 Ibid.
159 *New Witness*, May 24, 1918
160 *New Witness*, October 21, 1915
161 *New Witness*, March 10, 1922
162 *G. K.'s Weekly*, February 2, 1929
163 *New Witness*, June 20, 1919
164 "A Party Question," *The Queen of Seven Swords*
165 Ibid.
166 *New Witness*, March 2, 1923
167 Ibid.
168 *New Witness*, January 18, 1917
169 *New Witness*, September 30, 1921
170 *New Witness*, September 8, 1922
171 *New Witness*, August 18, 1922
172 *New Witness*, August 25, 1922
173 *New Witness*, January 18, 1917
174 *New Witness*, October 14, 1915
175 *New Witness*, April 27, 1923
176 *G. K.'s Weekly*, December 12, 1931
177 *G. K.'s Weekly*, October 11, 1934
178 *G. K.'s Weekly*, April 4, 1925
179 *G. K.'s Weekly*, April 11, 1925
180 *G. K.'s Weekly*, August 30, 1932
181 *G. K.'s Weekly*, June 13, 1925

182 *G. K.'s Weekly*, April 18, 1925
183 *G. K.'s Weekly*, July 19, 1930
184 *G. K.'s Weekly*, June 14, 1930
185 *G. K.'s Weekly*, July 12, 1930
186 *G. K.'s Weekly*, March 1933
187 *G. K.'s Weekly*, September 20, 1930
188 *G. K.'s Weekly*, September 27, 1930
189 *G. K.'s Weekly*, May 3, 1930
190 *G. K.'s Weekly*, December 15, 1928
191 *G. K.'s Weekly*, July 1929
192 *G. K.'s Weekly*, February 6, 1926
193 *G. K.'s Weekly*, September 14, 1929
194 *G. K.'s Weekly*, September 4, 1926
195 *G. K.'s Weekly*, March 9, 1929
196 *G. K.'s Weekly*, June 20, 1925
197 *G. K.'s Weekly*, December 7, 1929
198 "Figures in Fleet Street," *Autobiography*
199 "The God with the Golden Key," *Autobiography*
200 Ibid.
201 "The Blue Cross," *The Innocence of Father Brown*
202 "The Duel of Dr. Hirsch," *The Wisdom of Father Brown*
203 "The Miracle of Moon Crescent," *The Incredulity of Father Brown*
204 "The Dagger with Wings," *The Incredulity of Father Brown*
205 "The Oracle of the Dog," *The Incredulity of Father Brown*
206 I can't tell you where this one is from. It would be giving too
    much away.
207 Same problem. Solve it yourself.
208 "The Red Moon of Meru," *The Secret of Father Brown*
209 "The Worst Crime in the World," *The Secret of Father Brown*
210 "The Man with Two Beards," *The Secret of Father Brown*
211 "The Quick One," *The Scandal of Father Brown*
212 "The Scandal of Father Brown," *The Scandal of Father Brown*
213 "The Blast of the Book," *The Scandal of Father Brown*
214 Ibid.
215 "The Quick One," *The Scandal of Father Brown*
216 "The Point of a Pin," *The Scandal of Father Brown*
217 "The Quick One," *The Scandal of Father Brown*

218 "The Scandal of Father Brown," *The Scandal of Father Brown*
219 "The Insoluble Problem," *The Scandal of Father Brown*

The Saint?
1   "The War on Holidays," *Utopia of Usurers*
2   "At Overroads Door," *Return to Chesterton* (Maisie Ward)
3   "A Christmas Carol," *Collected Poetry*
4   *William Blake*
5   "The Maniac," *Orthodoxy*
6   "Serious but Never Solemn," *Return to Chesterton* (Maisie Ward)
7   Ibid.
8   "The Real Life of St. Thomas," *St. Thomas Aquinas*
9   *New York American*, February 3, 1934
10 "The Eternal Revolution," *Orthodoxy*
11 *Daily News*, September 24, 1910
12 *G. K.'s Weekly*, October 25, 1930
13 "The Eternal Revolution," *Orthodoxy*
14 "Two Voices," *The Napoleon of Notting Hill*
15 "The World St. Francis Found," *St. Francis of Assisi*
16 *Illustrated London News*, September 18, 1920
17 "The Eternal Revolution," *Orthodoxy*
18 *Daily News*, January 25, 1905
19 "The Wild Weddings—or The Polygamy Charge," *Manalive*
20 "The Book of Job," *G.K.C. as M.C.*
21 "The Notebook," *Gilbert Keith Chesterton* (Maisie Ward)
22 Ibid.
23 *Daily News*, March 1, 1901
24 "The Exception Proves the Rule," *The Catholic Church and Conversion*
25 "Tennyson," *A Handful of Authors*
26 *Daily News*, June 18, 1904
27 *Illustrated London News*, February 21, 1914
28 *G. K.'s Weekly*, August 8, 1935
29 "The Strange Music," *Collected Poetry*
30 "A Long Engagement," *Gilbert Keith Chesterton* (Maisie Ward)
31 "Portrait of a Young Man in Love," *Return to Chesterton* (Maisie Ward)

32 "Queen Victoria," *Varied Types*
33 "Charles II," *Twelve Types*
34 *Daily News*, September 5, 1904
35 *Daily News*, February 18, 1905
36 *Daily News*, November 17, 1906
37 "The Romance of Orthodoxy," *Orthodoxy*
38 "The Philosopher," *George Bernard Shaw*
39 *Dublin Review*, October 1910
40 *Illustrated London News*, February 24, 1912
41 "The Great Victorian Novelists," *Victorian Age in Literature*
42 *Illustrated London News*, November 21, 1914
43 *Divorce vs. Democracy* (Pamphlet)
44 "The Vista of Divorce," *The Superstition of Divorce*
45 *Illustrated London News*, June 5, 1920
46 *Illustrated London News*, March 24, 1923
47 *Illustrated London News*, March 21, 1925
48 *G. K.'s Weekly*, June 19, 1926
49 *Illustrated London News*, February 4, 1928
50 *G. K.'s Weekly*, July 6, 1929
51 *Illustrated London News*, November 15, 1930
52 *Illustrated London News*, September 24, 1932
53 *Illustrated London News*, December, 2 1933
54 *New York American*, June 3, 1933
55 *New York American*, February 9, 1935
56 "How to Be a Dunce," *Autobiography*
57 *Manchester Guardian*, January 21, 1907
58 *The Listener*, February 6, 1935
59 "Tolstoy," *Varied Types*
60 "The Strangest Story in the World," *The Everlasting Man*
61 "Conclusion," *The Everlasting Man*
62 Act II, *Time's Abstract and Brief Chronicle*
63 "Omar and the Sacred Vine," *Heretics*
64 Act 1, Sc.1, *The Surprise*
65 "The Face of Brass" (*Collected Works*, Vol. 14)
66 "The Notebook," *Gilbert Keith Chesterton* (Maisie Ward)
67 "The Last Parley," *The Ball and the Cross*
68 "The Ethics of Elfland," *Orthodoxy*

69 "A Child of the Snows," *Collected Poetry*

70 "Authority and the Adventurer," *Orthodoxy*

71 *Illustrated London News*, August 17, 1907

72 "Le Jongleur de Dieu," *St. Francis of Assisi*

73 *G. K. Chesterton: A Portrait* (Titterton)

74 "Vincent McNabb," *Gilbert!* April–May, 2005

75 *The World I Saw* (Maynard)

76 *Extension Magazine*, January 1927

77 Ibid.

78 Ibid.

79 "St. Thomas More," *The Well and the Shadows*